Out of the maze:

the clear-cut guide to business plans

By Peter Webster

Published by Proof Fairy Publishing: www.theprooffairy.com

First printing: 2013.

ISBN: 1-4823254-7-0

British Cataloguing Publication Data:
A catalogue record of this book is available from The British Library.

Also available on Kindle from Amazon.

Contents

How to use this guide

Take time to familiarise yourself with the contents of the guide before starting to write your plan, ideally reading the main text in full, completing the checklists and exercises and identifying the appendices you will want to come back to. You will then know which sections to refer to for help when dealing with a particular topic.

It is recommended that you use 'Appendix one – a suggested format for your business plan' as the template for your own plan; you can ignore any questions which you consider not relevant to your business.

If you are in doubt as to the meaning of any term used in the guide, you can refer to 'Appendix three – glossary' where you will find a definition of many of the terms commonly used in business.

The following checklists and exercises, once completed, will give you some of the material you will need to include in your business plan:

- Appendix five – possible tasks when running your business
- Appendix six- some examples of personality traits
- Appendix seven – some examples of business related skills
- Appendix nine – the cashflow forecast
- Appendix eleven – survival budget
- Appendix sixteen – breakeven and profit margins

- Appendix seventeen – the profit and loss forecast

You will find it helpful to build your own local support team (see page nine, advice and support), especially where you need specific financial or legal advice.

However, if you have any questions relating to the guide and the material contained within it, you can e mail to enquiries@pwadvice.co.uk and we will do our best to help you.

Introduction

There is much truth in the old saying 'You don't plan to fail, you simply fail to plan'. A practical and realistic plan can be the difference between long-term success and rapid failure. No one wants to see a business fail, but far too many do. There can be many reasons for this, such as overestimating demand and the price customers are prepared to pay; under-pricing your product or service; not being able to deliver on promises made to customers e.g. poor quality or failure to deliver on time; lack of ready cash to pay bills. Unfortunately, these are only a few of the problems which can occur, but most can be anticipated and dealt with at the planning stage – which brings us back to the business plan.

If you need to raise money to launch or grow your business you will have to complete a business plan – no bank or organisation will lend you money without one. However, the main reason for preparing a plan is 'self-defence'; in other words, cutting down the risks as far as possible. It will also remind you why you are doing what you are doing, keeping you on track and in control. If there is a problem you will see it coming. A business plan can be likened to planning a long, complex journey; you know where you are going and whether or not you have got there. A plan will help you to sell the idea of your business, not just to lenders but to suppliers and, of course, customers; it can also convince you that you have a viable business, giving you the confidence you need to move forward. Last but not least, the act of putting your business model into words will help to encourage realism – do the statements you have made stand up to examination? Where is the research and thinking to back up those statements?

The (market) research you carry out will be the key; you must be able to say 'yes' to this longwinded but totally relevant question - *are there enough customers out there who will come to you as opposed to your competition and who will pay your prices in sufficient numbers to give you the income you need?*

When complete your business plan will set out your business objectives and how they will be achieved; it will be a working document that you revisit and review at least annually. It will also give you an understanding of what works and what doesn't over time; you can do something about a problem if you know that you have one. It can also be argued that having a business plan will give you credibility, showing you to be professional and business-like and therefore to be taken seriously by banks, accountants, suppliers and even landlords.

As far as timing goes, ideally you should have your business plan in place well before you start your business (not least to prove its financial viability), reviewing it on a regular basis and updating it whenever you make any significant change in approach or direction. Two aspects of your plan will be crucial; firstly, marketing – how will potential customers know you exist, why will they buy from you, and more importantly, keep on buying from you? In plain terms – no customers, no business! Secondly, finance – what investment will you need and when? Will there be sufficient cash to pay your business bills and to give you the income you need on an on-going basis? What figures will help you to face facts and make decisions? Putting all of this together in a meaningful way will not be easy; however, the more thinking, planning and research you do now, the fewer problems there are likely to be later. The investment in time and effort should significantly improve your chances of surviving and thriving.

The plan format

Some points regarding completion.

There are many and varied formats for a business plan, some quite complex in detail and language, others less so. Unfortunately, there is no 'standard' format for a business plan, it is up to the individual to choose a version which suits their level of knowledge and understanding, and reflects their business model. This guide is based on the attached 'A suggested format for the business plan' – see Appendix one. This may look daunting, simply because of the number of questions posed; however, before you write a word you should delete or cross through any questions which are not relevant to your business model. *(Think carefully here; are you sure the question does not apply?)* That action then leaves you with a logical list of topics relevant to your business, which you need to address.

It may appear that the format goes into too much detail, but that is deliberate; the more questions dealt with 'up front', the less likely it is that there will be any nasty surprises later. The following material is designed to make completing a convincing business plan as painless as possible, by explaining what is meant by each question and by giving examples where this may be helpful. Do not attempt to complete too much in one go - break your work into manageable amounts; give yourself time to carry out the necessary research, to think and to revisit and review each section. Better to delay the start of your business and go into it with all the angles covered, than to cut corners and find yourself dealing with avoidable issues

One word of caution; you can always pay to have a business plan created for you, but with the best will in the world it will not truly reflect you and your approach to business. You are the best person to create your plan as you know, and can express, your business idea better than anyone else. Don't worry if your spelling and/or punctuation are not good – you are being judged on the strength of your business idea not on your command of English. (However, a professional looking plan does help.) There is a considerable amount of jargon which you are likely to come across in business – it may be helpful to refer to the attached glossary (Appendix three) early in the planning process.

While the guide is aimed mainly at businesses in the start-up stage, it is just as applicable to businesses which may be lacking in controls and/or a sense of direction.

You do not need to write detailed notes in full to answer all the relevant questions; in many cases a series of 'bullet points' will suffice, as long as the details are in your head so that you can provide a more detailed explanation if required. Don't spoil the flow of your plan by including too much data in the main text; summarise the data and create an appendix. For example, you could summarise the market research you have carried out – what, when and by whom, followed by your main conclusions and the action you will take as a result; the data on which all this is based will be contained in the appendix. You may feel that you do not need to include the answer to a specific question in your plan as it may not seem relevant to a potential lender; however, it is still worth thinking through the answer to ensure that you have covered all eventualities. Where possible, quote figures to back up your claims and provide a reference to the source; for instance, the population figures of local villages obtained from a local authority report.

Please note: this guide is designed to help you complete your business plan; it is not possible within its scope to give advice regarding the legal requirements of setting up a business, although some of the questions in the plan highlight what these might be. If in doubt, you *must* seek professional advice. (See Appendix Two – some sources of help and information.) Also, whilst every effort has been made to ensure the accuracy of the information in this guide, the author cannot accept any responsibility for errors or omissions.

To begin writing your plan, please refer to Appendix One – a suggested format for your business plan; *as a first step you will need to create a title page, showing your name, the name of your business and the date.*

Summary

This is the part of the plan that you will write last; as the title suggests, it is a summary of the crucial elements of your plan, designed to fully engage any reader. In some cases a potential lender may not read on beyond page one, if his or her interest is not aroused. In short, the summary is a statement setting out why the reader should believe in the business; so, once you have completed the rest of the plan you will need to briefly cover the following questions, but with as much conviction as possible.

Provide an overview of the business and its purpose.

Explain what the product or service is/will be and what makes it special as far as the customer is concerned (i.e. the USP – your 'unique selling point', see glossary), also any gap in the market which you have identified. In other words, why will there be a demand for what you do? You must differentiate your business from your competitors; you must give a reason why customers will come to you as opposed to your competition.

State your objectives – short, medium and long, both business and personal.

You could think of short term as being year one, medium term being to the end of year five and long term as beyond that. Define your business objectives for each time period, in terms of sales volume, turnover and size of customer base. (See glossary.) What figures must you achieve in each case? You could include any other objectives, such as the percentage of repeat business you are aiming to maintain.

Define your personal objectives in terms of the income you plan to draw from the business over time. In addition, state the benefits you hope to get from running your business such as job satisfaction, security or a better work/life balance.

Provide a brief statement as to how the business objectives will be achieved.

In other words why will you hit the targets set out in your objectives? Describe your customer profile (again see glossary), re-state your USP, state why you have concluded that there is a need for your product or service and *summarise* the marketing activities you will undertake to generate publicity and sales (what, when and budget) and why these methods will be effective.

The vision

Where do you see your business in five years time?

Describe what your business will look like in five years time in terms of the variety of products and services you will provide, your catchment area (see glossary), number of staff (if any), number of outlets, size of customer base, sales volume and turnover figures etc. Remember that this is a statement of your intentions or even an idealised picture; it is where you aim to be, but many things can occur to change this over a five year period. However, it will give the reader an idea of the scale of your ambitions. Don't be tempted to overdo this in a bid to make yourself seem more credible – if you plan to remain a one man/woman band then say so.

What is your motivation for starting this business?

Any potential backer will want to see how committed you are to making your business work; so what has motivated you to take what is a major step? Your reasons might be a combination of being your own boss, increased flexibility in terms of hours, making money for yourself rather than an employer, greater scope for using your creativity and imagination and probably most important of all – job satisfaction. These are all positive reasons for setting up your business – you may have others; what must come across is that this is something you have wanted to do and this is your chance to do it.

The structure

What legal structure have you chosen?

Simply state how your business will trade; will you be a sole trader, a partnership, a Limited Company, a Limited liability Partnership or a form of social enterprise? (See glossary.)

Why is this the right option?

State why the form of business status you have chosen is the right choice for you and your business. There are pluses and minuses for each of the forms of status and 'one size does not fit all'; see Appendix Four for some examples. However, if you are in *any* doubt as to the most suitable format for your business, you should take advice from an accountant or solicitor.

Do you need to register for VAT?

Simply state whether the business will or will not be VAT registered. You may have no choice but to register if your turnover will exceed the current registration threshold (see www.hmrc.gov.uk for the current figure); however, you can also register on a voluntary basis if this would be advantageous to you and your customers. Once again, if in doubt take advice from an accountant.

The people

What is the management structure?

This will only apply if there is more than one person running the business; if this is the case, then state their names and job titles.

What experience do you (they) have in running a business and of the product or service?

Again this will only apply if you have run a business in the past; if so, state the business and provide some history. How successful was it? If it failed, why was this? (A previous business failure does not mean that you cannot try again; in fact the lessons you will have learned will be an advantage when starting again. What are these lessons? How will they help you in your new venture?) If you have never run a business before then include a CV covering your employment history; this would be similar to one you would use when applying for a job. If you will be working in the same field as your previous employment, but now as a freelance, or you are turning a hobby into a business – then detail the knowledge and skills this experience has given you. Failing this, how did you/will you acquire the necessary knowledge and skills?

What roles are there? Who will carry them out?

State the various tasks which will need to be carried out on a day-to-day basis, (see Appendix Five for some examples) also who will be responsible for each task if there are others in the management team.

What skills are available and how will you capitalise on these?

No matter what your age and background there will be personality traits and skills which you will have acquired over time and which will be transferable to your new business. (See Appendices Six and Seven for some examples.) Write two or three short paragraphs describing what you can 'bring to the party' and how these traits/skills can help make you successful. Don't be too modest – if you are good at something then say so. In effect, you are selling yourself to the reader, giving them confidence in you. This exercise will also give you confidence, by reminding you of your abilities; most people underestimate themselves, believing that as they have never run a business before they have nothing to build on.

What skills gaps/weaknesses are there and how fill you fill these?

Be honest with yourself and realistic; state any weak areas as far as your personality and skills are concerned – for instance, having no head for figures, being a poor time keeper etc. What actions will you take to plug the gaps in terms of training or outside help, such as a bookkeeper, accountant or virtual assistant? There is no problem with outsourcing; the problem arises when you ignore a gap and do nothing about filling it.

Advice and support

What does your support team consist of?

One of the dangers of self-employment is the feeling of isolation that can build up; but you are not alone, there are people who can help you albeit usually at some cost. Most businesses will use an accountant and sometimes a solicitor; you will need a business bank account – who is your account manager? You can join a trade or professional body or a networking group and maybe use sub-contractors to cope with jobs too big to manage on your own. If you have any of these relationships set up, then state the name.

How will they help you be successful?

State how your support team will provide backup and plug any gaps in your skill set or free you up to concentrate on the most important aspect of your business – your customers. It may also be cost effective to go outside for help and support; time is money and specialists may be able to complete jobs far faster than you can when doing it yourself, as well as achieving a better result.

Red tape

What legal requirements must you comply with?

All businesses are bound to some extent by rules and regulations. To begin with you must register your business so that the relevant authorities know that you are trading and will therefore be liable to file accounts and pay tax. For information on this see www.hmrc.gov.uk or www.companieshouse.gov.uk; once again, if in doubt, talk to an accountant or solicitor. Other regulations which might affect you cover: sales of goods and services (including distance selling e.g. the internet), employment law, the minimum wage, the environment and waste disposal, fair and unfair terms and conditions, late payment of bills etc. Once again, if you are in any doubt check with your local Trading Standards office or a solicitor. An easier and possibly cheaper way to find out exactly which rules and regulations affect you might be to join a trade or professional body or to purchase the relevant Business Opportunity Profile from www.scavenger.net (see Appendix Two – some sources of help and information). These profiles and the accompanying Business Information Factsheets are extremely useful in summarising what you must do to comply with the law in a particular business as well as providing much other relevant information, such as the cost of setting up and insurance requirements. Having researched the legal requirements, then state which regulations apply to your business and briefly what you have done/will do to comply.

Do you need a licence?

Not all businesses do, but it is wise to check using the sources given for the previous question. If applicable, state the type of licence you require and the steps you have taken/will take to acquire it.

Do you need patent, trade mark, design or copyright protection?

All of these come under the heading of intellectual property; in other words, protecting the tangible aspects of your business idea. These could have considerable value, for instance if you are an inventor, a writer or musician. For guidance on what can be protected and how to go about obtaining protection, see www.ipo.gov.uk which is the website of the Intellectual Property Office. If applicable state the type of material you need to protect and the steps you have taken/will take to obtain the necessary protection.

What are the health and safety requirements?

You have a duty to protect your staff, customers, suppliers and sub-contractors from harm; you also have a duty to yourself. If you are off work due to an avoidable accident you will lose money and possibly your hard-earned customer base, if you cannot work long term. For guidance on how health and safety legislation affects a business of your size (in terms of employees) and type of trade, visit the website of the Health and Safety Executive (www.hse.gov.uk). Alternatively ask your trade or professional body or visit the Business Link website (www.businesslink.gov.uk). State any specific requirements and what you have done/will do to comply with them.

Have you carried out a risk assessment? What policies need to be written?

Based on your answer to the above question, state whether these need to be written and, if so, what has been/ will be done. You might consider attaching these as appendices, if applicable.

What insurances are required for the business and for you?

Some forms of business insurance are required by law and some are advisable; it is very risky to be without insurance or to be under insured. For advice on this, speak to an insurance broker or refer to the relevant Business Opportunity Profile from Scavenger. Better still, if you are a member of a trade or professional body you might be able to buy the necessary insurances from them; these could not only be more affordable but also better tailored to the risks you face in your particular business. State the insurance cover you need and what has been/will be done to obtain it. Don't forget that once you start working for yourself you may no longer be saving, investing in a pension or be covered against the risk of serious illness; state any actions you have taken/will take to protect yourself in future.

The basics

What is/are the product(s) or service(s) in detail?

Describe precisely what you will be selling in terms of what it is, what it does, what is involved in its production or service delivery, level of quality and your ability to adapt to changes in demand. If there are a variety of products or services, describe each one as above but also detail how these products or services relate to and complement each other, particularly from a prospective customer's point of view. Can one product or service be sold 'on the back of' another? State how consistency can be achieved and maintained in terms of quality, design, performance and price levels.

What contribution will each make?

This question will only be applicable where you are selling a number of products or services. Based on your market research and pricing decisions (see the sections on marketing and finance), set out the percentage of total profit each product or service will contribute. This will demonstrate whether it is worth producing a particular product or delivering a particular service; does everything you sell make a meaningful contribution to your turnover and profit? If not, why sell it? You could also show this as the percentage of sales volume i.e. items or services sold rather than pounds.

What further products or services are being developed?

All products and services will 'run out of steam' over time; they will become less attractive to customers as fashions and technology change, as spending power increases or decreases and as competition intensifies. State what you will do in the long term to address this issue, such as introducing new products or services or refreshing these or by learning new skills.

What are the timescales and costs involved?

Set out when you plan to introduce new products or services or update these, together with any expenses you will incur as a result. State how these planned changes will help to keep existing customers and attract new ones. Don't forget to include any planned expenditure in your cashflow. (See the section on finance.)

The market

What, when and how has market research been done, both desk and field? (See glossary.)

Your research will provide the answers to all the questions in this section; it is a vital activity but can appear daunting; a lot of work has to be done before you can say that you have a viable business. There should be no short cuts – trusting that 'it will be alright on the night' is not the answer. The steps you take might be:

- One – decide which questions you must answer. (These can be taken directly from this document coupled with Appendix One.)
- Two – decide where you might look for the answers; see 'Appendix Eight - some sources for market research', which details some of the people, organisations and materials that you might refer to.
- Three - set aside time and begin your research; this could be likened to detective work, in that you will be sifting through large amounts of data in search of facts and information.

Detail the types of research and sources you have used in your research and the period(s) of time over which the research was carried out.

What are the main conclusions?

Set out the *main facts* you have established regarding the prospects for your business i.e. the size of the market for your product or service in total and your possible market share, in terms of sales volume and turnover. State the source of these figures where you can and refer to the answers to other questions where relevant. Can you show that the turnover achievable will be sufficient to pay your business expenses, to give you a reasonable standard of living and leave you with a profit? Do this by comparing your planned turnover to the costs you have calculated, as set out in your cashflow.

Where is the evidence for these conclusions?

State where the evidence to back up your claims can be found within the sections of your plan. Remember that where you have compiled large amounts of research data, for instance a list of competitors together with their strengths and weaknesses and prices, or lists of potential customers, you should put these into appendices rather than spoil the flow of your plan.

Has the need been established?

State why you believe the market you are entering is currently underserved or your competition cannot or will not provide the service levels or prices that customers want. Refer to any research which shows this to be the case.

Is this a growing market? Is there room for your business?

Set out any figures which show a pattern of growth in your type of business over a number of years and the potential for future growth. If the figures show that the market is shrinking, explain how you will be able to survive this downturn and why you are persevering in the face of this information. Does your business have a future?

What economic, legislative and other factors have been taken into account?

Are there any identifiable positive or negative effects on your business due to current economic factors, planned or sudden changes in legislation or developments in technology? If so, state what these might be and what actions you will take to mitigate any negative effects or to take advantage of any which are positive?

If test selling has been carried out, what has been the reaction?

You may have already 'dipped a toe in the water' by making a few sales; either by carrying out some test marketing – maybe by placing a one-off advertisement and measuring the response, or because people who have heard what you are doing have approached you. Either way, if you have already made sales, this is good evidence that what you do sells and that you can do the selling. Quote any figures or examples which detail sales already made.

Is this a fashion or seasonal item? What will you do when business is quiet?

Nearly every type of business is seasonal; you will have ups and downs in income and expenditure. This seasonality should be reflected in your cashflow, to demonstrate that you can pay your way over time. (See Appendix Nine – the cashflow forecast, for an illustration of this.) Ideally you will have another source of income in the form of other products or services or even a part-time job, if there might be a significant shortfall at any time during the year. Another solution might be to hold a cash sum in your business bank account, which will tide you over when income drops. State how you will deal with those times when money is short.

What is the level of customer awareness of the product/service?

Customers tend to avoid new and unfamiliar products or services – why should they buy what they don't understand or feel that they need? If this could be true of your product or service then state what you will do to create awareness through your marketing activities and to highlight the aspect of your product or service which will persuade customers to try something new or to switch to you as a supplier. Remember that customers do not buy what you sell for what it is, they buy it for what it can do for them. There are many things which could motivate a purchase and many aspects of you or your business which they might warm to; which of these apply to your business and why? (See 'Appendix Ten – reasons to buy' for some examples.)

What are the marketing objectives – sales volume, turnover, margins, number of customers?

State the target figures which you have arrived at as a result of your market research for each of the above. These are the figures which put you in control of your business; they need to be specific, quantifiable, measureable and time defined. You will then know whether or not you are on target, and if not, that you need to take action. If you don't know that you have a problem, it may be too late to do anything about it when you do eventually find out.

What is the number of sales times price required to break even?

One of the questions you may really struggle with is the level of sales you might achieve; a much more down-to-earth way to establish a sales figure is to add together your total business expenses for the year (as detailed in your cashflow) and your survival budget. (See glossary and Appendix Eleven.) This, put crudely, is your breakeven; it is what you *must* do in terms of sales just to pay the bills. Divide this figure by the average price you anticipate charging; this will give you the number of sales you *must* make in the year – divide by twelve to obtain your monthly target. You could calculate a weekly or even a daily target if you want to be in total control regarding progress, or lack of it. The good thing about this approach is that you are dealing in facts, so the figures are believable; your marketing plan must then set out how it will be possible to achieve these figures.

What is the customer profile? Are there identified clients or an order book?

You can't be all things to all men, neither can you please all of the people all of the time. However you phrase it, this is telling you that you must specifically target your prospective customers; using a 'scattergun' approach to the advertising and promotion that you do will only result in a lot of wasted money and effort. Therefore you must define the type or types of customers you will be selling to; this enables you to use the most effective methods of advertising and promotion and to choose the wording and images your customers are most likely to respond to.

For instance, are you selling to businesses or to private customers, or both? Do you have to please not just your customer but their customers as well? So, define your target audience, or in the jargon, your customer profile; see Appendix Twelve for some of the ways in which you might categorise your customers and Appendix Thirteen for some examples of the type of profile you might arrive at.

On the other hand, you may have already started to build a client base – for instance a hairdresser may take his or her clients with him or her when he or she goes freelance. (Be aware that this could be problematic if there is a clause in his/her contract which prevents this.) If you are buying an existing business there will be an established customer base; if you are buying a franchise, the franchisor may guarantee to provide you with a number of customers at the outset. Any of these situations would be good news as you are more likely to achieve a reasonable and defined income from the start. State what your customer base consists of in terms of numbers and profile, include any related sales figures in your cashflow and name names where possible e.g. where you have made sales to, or formed a relationship with, customers.

What is the level of competition? Who, where and what? What are their strengths and weaknesses? What must you do to capitalise on your strengths and to catch up where necessary?

Almost certainly there are others out there doing what you are doing, some better, some the same and some not so well; without being over dramatic, it is a case of survival of the fittest. You are not only concerned with sales today, you should be thinking long term – it's all about reputation;

businesses which can build a loyal customer base, bringing in repeat business and new customers, will save much time, money and stress. Finding a new customer can cost four or five times more than it costs to retain an existing customer.

So list all the identifiable competition within your catchment area (this could be worldwide if you are trading on the web), by name, by location and by the products or services they offer. Try to look at them objectively – what do they do well? Is there anything you can learn from them and build into your way of working? Are there weaknesses in what they do or how they do it, as far as their customers are concerned? If so, what can you do to capitalise on these? You are looking for ways to play to your strengths and to minimise any weaknesses. There will be a great deal of detail related to this question, so summarise your findings in the main text and attach an appendix with the supporting information. There are a number of ways in which you can identify competitors and research their strengths and weaknesses – see Appendix Fourteen for some examples.

What is your USP? What other features and advantages can you define? Where can you 'go the extra mile'?

This follows on naturally from the previous question. It is essential to differentiate yourself from your competitors; what can you do that others can't, won't or don't do? Where can you specialise or carve out a niche for yourself in the marketplace? By creating a USP (Unique Selling Point) you will give customers a reason to beat a path to your door, rather than that of your competition; In short, what will make you stand out from the crowd?

Once this has been decided, your USP will feature prominently in all of your publicity material and your website; customers need to know from the outset who you are, what you do and what makes you special. Having compared yourself to the competition, where do you believe your greatest strength lies? Don't forget that people are vital in any business – you could be the USP of your business, simply because of the person you are and the approach you take to your customers; any business is based on relationships. If customers do not warm to you they are less likely to buy and to provide repeat business.

In addition to your USP, identify and list any features of your product or service and the potential advantages they offer to your customers. (See 'feature, advantage and benefit' in the glossary.) These will be the basis of your product knowledge and will be used in the selling process in addition to your USP; identifying them will also give you confidence in your product or service – it is much easier to sell if you can really believe in what you do.

'Going the extra mile' means exceeding customer expectations, which in turn helps to build your reputation and that valuable repeat business. What practical steps can you take on a day-to-day basis to ensure that you always do the best job you can? These actions need to be specific, not just vague aspirations; many businesses claim to provide high levels of service and customer care, but far too often this is little more than 'lip service'.

What does your marketing plan consist of? Methods of advertising and promotion – what, where and when? At what cost?

Obviously if nobody knows that you are out there, then you will have no business; bearing in mind your customer profile, which methods of advertising and promotion will you use to get your message across? List these and detail where they will appear – such as specific magazines – and when they will appear. Bear in mind publication dates and deadlines. Where promotion is concerned, what actions will you be taking and when? Cost these activities and include this in your cashflow as your budget for marketing

Do you have a portfolio or case studies to support your sales effort?

As they say 'a picture speaks a thousand words'; it is much easier to get your message across if you have some form of visual aid – photos, plans, storyboards etc. Do you have any of these to help a customer understand your product or service and its advantages? When it comes to selling a service it can be very difficult to convey what difference your service could make to your customer; a solution might be to prepare a number of short case studies setting out details of work you have carried out in the past. These should cover the nature of the problem or opportunity you worked on, some of your methodology (without giving away too much), and most importantly, what was achieved as a result of your intervention. If you can quote figures, then so much the better; e.g. the decrease in the number of customer complaints or wastage, or the increase in profitability etc.

Simply state the visual aids or case studies you have at your disposal.

What corporate image will be projected and how? (Colour, logo, name, typefaces, signage, uniforms etc.)

How do you want your customers to see you? A business majoring on quality needs to reinforce the message with a business-like and professional image; look around at your competition and the marketplace in general – what aspects of design will help to convey the image you are aiming for? The really important aspect of this is consistency; whatever form of corporate image you choose, it should run through all your promotional material, from business card to website. The business name should ideally reflect what the business does or its ideals and values. State the actions you will take to create your desired image.

What is/are the trading pattern/hours?

Simply state when customers will be able to access your business; are you available twenty four/seven, weekends or evenings? Bear in mind local trading hours, access to premises, convenience to customers and the effect on your personal life.

What are the quality criteria and methods of measurement?

How will you know whether you are doing a good job as far as your customers are concerned? Define any standards that you are aiming for e.g. '95% satisfied customers', 'no more than 3% returns' or 'repeat business to be 45% of the total' etc. Then specify the form of follow-up/checks you will implement, together with the frequency – for example, sending out a customer satisfaction questionnaire at least annually.

What is the goodwill policy re complaints and service levels?

Hopefully, you will have few dissatisfied customers, but if you do have a problem you can turn a very unhappy customer into one who is singing your praises if their complaint is well handled. Define who will deal with any dissatisfied customers, the actions which could be taken to resolve the problem and what form of compensation (if any) you are prepared to offer.

What selling and negotiation skills are available?

Having a good product or service is not enough – you need to be able to persuade customers to willingly part with their money. Do you have any experience of selling? How confident are you in yourself and your product? How good are you with words, both written and spoken? State your level of skill or who in your business is responsible for selling if not you; if the skills are lacking do you need training or will you recruit a salesperson or agent?

What are the terms and conditions of trading?

It is very important that both you and your customer are clear as to what is involved in any transaction, especially when it comes to payment. It is wise to document the details of any work you undertake and to obtain your customer's signature once everything is agreed. Back this up with a statement of your terms and conditions; you can ask a solicitor to draw these up, download a standard template from the internet or possibly obtain a recommended version from your trade or professional body. Simply state that your terms and conditions have been/will be documented and perhaps attach a copy if this is available.

Suppliers

These next few questions will not apply if you do not purchase stock or materials; however, you could substitute 'sub-contractor' for 'supplier' if you will use them.

Who and where are your suppliers?

Your suppliers can be very important to your business; you cannot afford to let your customers down because your suppliers turn out to be unreliable. State the types of stock or materials that you will be buying and the suppliers you have decided to work with.

Why are you using them?

State what has persuaded you to go with these suppliers e.g. range, price, reliability, reputation, brand image etc. (Have you checked their service levels with any of their existing customers? Have you looked them up on the Companies House website if they are a limited company?)

Do you have a fall back plan in case of supplier failure?

If despite all your efforts a supplier lets you down, do you have a backup? If so, who is it? Customers are not impressed if you blame your failure to deliver on your suppliers even if it is the suppliers fault – they are dealing with you, not your supplier.

What are their terms and conditions?

Have you read the 'small print' in your suppliers' terms and conditions? If so, are these terms and conditions acceptable and helpful in the way that you run your business? How long have you got to settle a bill? Will they charge interest on late payment? State any issues you may have with their terms and conditions and the steps you will take to mitigate the problem. Remember that payment terms will be reflected in your cashflow, which will need to show when bills are paid based on any payment terms agreed; for example, if you have negotiated thirty days credit, the invoice will be paid a month after the goods have been delivered and invoiced.

What stock levels will you carry and what are the controls?

Too much stock ties up your cash, too little stock loses sales. Research and document your ideal stock levels (this will also help save time when you place the orders); if you have a shop or warehouse it is helpful to draw up both a floor and wall plan, showing what stock will go where. This will help with the accuracy of your ordering and when stock is delivered both you and your staff will already know where it is to be located. Also state the system you will use to monitor sales and re-order stock, so that you always maintain your planned stock levels.

Distribution

These questions will only apply if you have to get your products to your customers.

What products will you need to distribute and how will this be done?

Simply state the type of products you will need to distribute and the methods/suppliers you have chosen to do this.

What are the costs and time scales?

Calculate the cost of distribution for each product, bearing in mind the distances and weights which may be involved; either build this into your cost price (see Appendix Fifteen – costing examples), or quote this as an addition to your basic price in which case you will have to clearly show this as an add-on to avoid any confusion as far as your customers are concerned.

Are there any security issues?

If you are distributing high value or fragile items will these be properly insured and/or packed? If using a carrier are there problems with their terms and conditions – are you fully covered if goods are lost or damaged? State the arrangements you have made/will make to minimise any losses and to keep track of deliveries whilst in transit, also to obtain proof of delivery.

Finance

It may be wise to refer back to the glossary before starting on this section, to help in translating the necessary jargon.

What are the calculations for breakeven, gross and net profit?

Anyone you approach for funding will want to see these figures; you will also need these figures in order to know whether your business is viable and to enable you to stay in control. For help with these calculations see the examples and exercises contained in Appendix Sixteen – breakeven and profit margins exercise.

Is there a cashflow forecast? Does this need to cover years two and three?

The cashflow and the profit and loss forecasts are crucial documents; without them you cannot demonstrate your ability to pay bills over time and to pay yourself a living wage while generating profit, thus enabling you to grow your business. Include your cashflow as an appendix (see the example and exercise contained in Appendix Nine – cashflow forecast, which you should attempt before creating your own); if you are planning to borrow a significant sum of money, then you should complete a cashflow for years two and three as well as year one.

Is a profit and loss included?

The cashflow will help in many ways when it comes to understanding and controlling the finances of your business, however it will not tell you whether you will make a profit. In other words, will the income you generate in the year more than cover the cost of generating that income? Attach your profit and loss forecast as an appendix. (See the example and exercise contained in Appendix Seventeen – profit and loss forecast, which you should attempt before creating your own.)

How have prices been calculated? How do they compare with the competition and why are there differences?

This question harks back to your market research; ideally you will set out your price (or prices), showing comparisons with your competition. Explain why you have decided to set your price/s at the same level, or higher or lower than your competition – what is the rationale for the difference? Remember that you can lose business by appearing to be too cheap; if your price seems to be 'too good to be true, then customers may walk away. If you are claiming that your product or service is of premium quality then your price should reflect this. There are many factors which might lead you to raise or lower your price – see 'Appendix Eighteen – pricing, factors to consider' for some thoughts regarding this decision. Basically, you will need to compare the strengths and weaknesses of your product or service with those of your competitors. If yours has more strengths overall than that of your competitors, then you will charge more than them; if you have some catching up to do, then you will charge the same or less. Be as objective as you can and give your competitors credit where it is due.

How have your costings been calculated? Do these include your drawings? (Survival budget.)

Your profit is the difference between your sales and the cost of generating those sales, so calculating your costs accurately is another very important activity. You must include any direct costs, overheads, salary or drawings and provision for tax and VAT (whether VAT registered or not, remember you are being charged VAT on all your purchases, which in turn must be passed on to your customers as part of your final selling price). In effect you are building a contribution to each type of expense into your cost price, so that every time you make a sale you recover a percentage of your direct costs, drawings etc. The problem is knowing how much this should be in actual cash terms. Through your research you need to be able to predict two sets of figures: firstly, the total direct costs, the total overheads and your survival budget (making provision for the tax you will have to pay). Secondly, the number of sales you expect to make during the year. Divide the number of sales into each total to give you the cost element for that category of expense. So, for example, if your total overheads will come to £13,500 for the year and your sales target is 250, then the cost element just to cover your overheads would be £54. Similarly, if you plan to pay yourself an income of £28,000 (again having made provision to pay your tax bill), then your cost will include £112 just to cover your income. (£28000 ÷ 250). This approach will give you a reasonably accurate costing based on your research and predictions; once in business you can review your costs and sales figures and alter your cost price accordingly. Once you have accurate costings you can immediately see whether your prices more than cover these costs and therefore whether you will make a profit. Services and products can be costed in ways other than that shown above; see the examples contained in Appendix Fifteen which may be of help when calculating your costs.

What are your personal financial objectives?

Hopefully your reasons for starting or running a business are not purely financial; however, you need to be able to maintain your standard of living and, ideally, improve it. Go back through your bank and credit card statements and your utility bills then calculate your weekly and monthly personal and household expenses, totalling these for the year. (See 'Appendix Eleven – survival budget' for an example of how you might set out these expenses.) This exercise will tell you the minimum you will need to take in drawings or salary – include the figures in your cashflow, as 'drawings' if you are a sole trader or partner or as PAYE if you run a limited company. Don't forget to include any tax and National Insurance you will have to pay.

What books are kept and by whom?

All businesses must keep proper records detailing all sales and expenses; if in doubt as to what this entails either consult the HMRC website or speak to an accountant. Records can be electronic or hard copy, but all back up paperwork must be retained for a defined period. Properly kept records will save you time and money and help to avoid any possible problems with the tax man; state how your records will be kept and who is responsible for their upkeep and the filing of tax returns.

What credit control procedures are in place?

This will only apply if you offer credit facilities to your customers i.e. you invoice and wait to be paid. You will have bills to pay, therefore it is vital that you are paid on time and in full. Obvious precautions include putting all your agreements in writing and agreeing your terms and conditions with your customers before carrying out work; talk to a solicitor, to your trade or professional body or see www.payontime.co.uk for guidance. State how you will minimise the risks of late or non-payment and what procedures you will follow should these arise.

What funding is required and what is it for? What is your contribution and what percentage is this of the total?

List everything you need in the way of equipment or services to start and run your business; include money to cover your living expenses until cash comes in from sales. If funds are limited then concentrate on what is essential rather than desirable. Any expenses and the timing of them should be included in your cashflow. If you need to borrow to fund these expenses then state the amount that you need to borrow, how much you can contribute to the total expenditure and what percentage of the total this represents. The greater your contribution, the less risk to any lender and therefore a better chance of obtaining the funds you need.

Are there any other sources of funding, if so, what has been secured?

If there is any other source of lending or income that will support your business, then state what this is; for instance, borrowing from family members or taking a part time job.

State whether this income has been secured and if so, include any money coming in and any repayments going out in your cashflow.

What repayments are required and when? Does the cashflow support this?

If you will be repaying a loan or leasing, then show the timing of any payments in your cashflow, which needs to demonstrate that these are affordable i.e. that sufficient cash will always be available to make these payments on a monthly basis. *Without this evidence lenders will not lend and you cannot risk borrowing.*

What security do you have and what level of risk can you accept?

State any assets you can offer as security against a loan, if this would be required by a potential lender. Consider any assets you are *not* prepared to offer (your home, for instance), which might mean refusing the offer of a loan if you felt the risk was too great.

Is there a fall back plan/exit strategy in place?

State the action you might take if, despite your best efforts, the business does not take off. What is 'plan B'? What could you do to get yourself back on your feet? Develop the business in a different direction? Downsize the idea? Take a job?

What management information is required and when? What controls are in place?

State the figures that you need, to be able to understand, control and manage your business (such as breakeven, profit margins, percentage of returns, staff turnover etc.), how these will be collected and how often reviewed.

Staffing

You can ignore this section if you will not employ staff now or in the future, however, even if you are a one man/woman band there may be some relevance – for example, your own training needs. And while you would not employ any more staff than necessary, there may be instances where you cannot manage on your own – for example running a shop.

What numbers are required, what are their roles and what skills are required? Are the right type of staff available?

State how many staff you will need to recruit, their job titles and any specific personality traits or skills which are required. What will you do if staff possessing the desired skills or traits are hard to find?

What is the pattern for staff coverage?

State the opening times of the business and the number of staff required at different times of the day or days of the week, according to your predicted sales pattern. The resulting wage bill must of course be included in your cashflow under wages, salary or simply PAYE.

What training will they need? How, when and by whom will this be delivered and at what cost?

Investing time and money in your staff pays dividends – your business is only as good as the weakest member of staff. State any training they will require to enable them to perform to their best, both induction and ongoing training. State how and when it will be delivered and if there is an associated cost, show this in your cashflow. You could set the training programme out as a matrix, showing subjects to be covered together with timings.

How, when and at what cost will they be recruited?

State the methods or agencies that you will use to find the right staff and the timing of any recruitment drive; include any costs in your cashflow.

What rates will need to be paid? What are the terms and conditions and what facilities will be provided?

Research the 'going rate' for the type of work you are offering, looking at the employment pages in newspapers and talking to your local Employment Service. Calculate the likely wage bill and include this in your cashflow, as stated above. Talk to a solicitor or go on line to obtain a set of employment terms and conditions and to obtain up-to-date information on employment law. State the facilities you will provide for your staff, bearing in mind health and safety requirements.

What systems are in place for discipline, grievance, appraisal, motivation and development?

To get the best out of your staff, they need to feel that they have been treated fairly; that is, rewarded or praised when they have done well and taken to task when things have gone wrong. Discipline especially is a very complex area – talk to a solicitor or a personnel professional for advice on the procedures that you should put in place and follow. State where you will go for help when guidance is required and outline any systems in place to help recognise performance and training needs. Any cost incurred as a result of the above will of course need to be included in your cashflow.

How will staff be presented?

If your staff will be customer facing they will need to look the part i.e. professional and easily identifiable. State any requirements regarding presentation; if a uniform is to provided, state what this will consist of.

Premises

Even if you plan to work from home some of the following questions will apply to you, as you will need to create a working environment where you can be most productive. You will also need to consider any issues which may arise from working from home.

What type of premises are required and where?

Simply state the purpose e.g. retail, office, production or distribution, together with the planned location.

What is important in terms of facilities, access, image and neighbours?

List the essentials related to the above, together with any desirable criteria, to enable you to identify the premises closest to your ideal when conducting your property search. If you have already identified premises, state why these will suit your needs.

Are the premises leased or owned? What are the terms and cost involved?

If you have already found premises, state whether these are leased or owned. (Note: you are strongly advised to seek legal advice before signing a lease.) State whether there are specific terms which you must comply with, together with any costs involved such as rent, business rates, buildings insurance, cost of maintenance, waste disposal, legal fees etc. As usual, include all these costs in your cashflow.

If working from home, what resources are required and how can a working environment be created?

State the equipment you will need, or already possess, to enable you to work efficiently from home – this could include office furniture as well as IT equipment. (Note: the value of this equipment may affect your contents insurance.) Also state the steps you can take to enable you to work undisturbed and to have your paperwork and reference material to hand.

Are there issues relating to image, planning or tax?

There may be issues related to your mortgage or lease terms, buildings and contents insurance, taxation, planning or the requirement to pay business rates. If in doubt it is wise to consult your local authority, accountant, mortgage and insurance provider or landlord. State any issues arising and any steps you have taken/will take to deal with them.

Resources

What resources are needed in the start-up phase and in the future?

You may have covered some or all of this in the answers to previous questions; if not, then list all the equipment and services you will need to buy in and when you plan to purchase them. Once again, cost these and include them in your cashflow, on the basis of when the spending will take place i.e. before or after you start to trade.

What is the justification for purchase?

If you are purchasing an item which is of considerable value or is significantly more expensive than available alternatives, then state what this is and the reason why the item is needed or why you have opted for the more expensive version.

What is the total cost and how will they be funded/purchased?

State the total cost of all the equipment and services you will need (again including all of these costs in your cashflow), and where the funds will come from. Also state whether the equipment will be owned outright or leased.

What is the type and value of any assets already owned?

If you already possess suitable equipment which you will use in your business, then state what this is and its approximate current value. (This will be helpful when claiming any capital allowances.)

Information technology

What will any system be used for i.e. tasks to be performed?

Think about your job description; which tasks will be carried out using your computer? Which tasks could be made simpler/faster by using your computer? For example bookkeeping, stock control or customer records. List these.

What hardware and software will be required and how will this be supported?

Based on the answers to the questions above, specify the hardware and software you will need to enable you to carry out these tasks; this will give you the tools you need and help to avoid spending money on technology you will not use. Also state what you will do if you encounter problems; will you rely on your providers or use an IT specialist to deal with your problem?

What is the level of familiarity and what training will be required?

Do you need training to enable you to use your hardware and software to advantage? If so what will this consist of and where and how can you obtain it?

What security systems are in place? How will information be backed up?

Simply state what systems and hardware are in place to ensure that your data is protected and to prevent anyone gaining access to your computer. If you are trading over the internet how can you be sure that your transactions are safe? What practical steps have you taken to back up your data?

How will customers be able to contact the business?

You will want to make it as easy as possible for customers to contact you in order to do business and also to avoid the problem of missed calls; if telephone calls or e mails are not answered, customers will inevitably go elsewhere. State the ways in which customers will be able to contact you, including out of normal business hours. You might consider using a virtual office service (see glossary) if there will be times when you cannot be available to answer calls e.g. when talking to a customer or taking a holiday.

Will the business have a website, if so, for what purpose? Who will build this, when at what cost? How will the site be promoted and found?

Most customers will expect your business to have a website and will often want to visit this before making contact; therefore, its look, content and ease of use will be crucial, also how quickly it can be found by search engines. Has it been designed from the point of view of the user, rather than yours or your web designer? State what your website will be designed to do e.g. act as a 'shop window' or allow you to take payments over the internet; also state who will design, build and maintain the site to ensure that it makes the most effective marketing statement possible and complies with any legal requirements. Include the cost of building and maintaining your site in your cashflow and state what will be done to draw customers to it.

Existing businesses

This section obviously only applies to businesses which have been trading for a reasonable period of time; lenders will want to look at the 'track record' in order to understand the degree of risk and how any investment will help to grow the business, or keep it afloat if there is a short term problem.

What was the start date and what has been the history?

Put together a short summary of the progress and achievements of your business since its start date; be as honest and objective as possible.

What is the current situation? (SWOT analysis.)

State where the business now stands in the market place, by listing its current strengths and possible weaknesses, together with any opportunities to be grasped or any threats to be dealt with.

What is the current client base? What is the size of the order book?

State the current customer profile(s) and the size of your customer base; also calculate the value of all business/orders currently outstanding, showing how much cash will come in over the next few months.

Are profit and loss figures provided to cover the last three years?

Include as appendices, copies of any profit and loss statements you have going back over three years if these are available; if you have been trading for less than a year, create a profit and loss covering the months you have been trading and be prepared to open your books to support these figures.

Is a balance sheet available?

Again, include as an appendix any up-to-date balance sheet you have available, to demonstrate the value of any business assets which could be used as security.

An end note

That's all the questions listed in the Suggested Format for a Business Plan dealt with; if you complete a plan based on these questions there will not be much left to chance and you should have a clear sense of direction and more confidence in your ability to build a viable business. Running a business is challenging, but as long as things go reasonably well for you, not only will you generate an income, but hopefully, a great deal of job satisfaction. Good luck with your endeavours.

Out of the Maze:
the clear-cut guide to business plans

Appendices section

To download all the forms and tables in Out of the maze,

as well as a working cash flow forecast, visit

www.outofthemaze.biz/book-downloads

and use the password "churchill" (all lower case)

Out of the maze - appendix one

A SUGGESTED FORMAT FOR A BUSINESS PLAN

Summary

- An overview of the business and its purpose
- A brief statement as to how the business objectives will be achieved

The vision

- State your objectives – short, medium and long term, both business and personal?
- What is your motivation for starting this business?

The structure

- What legal structure have you chosen?
- Why is this the right option?
- Do you need to register for VAT?

The people

- What is the management structure?
- What experience do you (they) have in running a business and of the product or service?
- What roles are there, who will carry them out and why?
- What skills are available and how will you capitalise on these?

- What skill gaps/weaknesses are there and how will you fill these?

Advice and support

- What does your support team consist of? Accountant, solicitor, bankers, specialists and statutory bodies.
- How will they help you be successful?

Red tape

- What legal requirements must you comply with?
- Do you need a licence?
- Do you need patent, trade marks, design or copyright protection?
- What are the health and safety requirements?
- Have you carried out a risk assessment?
- What policies need to be written?
- What insurances are required for the business and for you?

The basics

- What is/are the product(s) or service(s) in detail?
- What contribution to profit will each make?
- What further products/services are being developed?
- What are the timescales and costs involved?

The market

- What, when and how has market research been done, both desk and field?

- What are the main conclusions?
- Where is the evidence for these conclusions? (Place detailed data in appendices.)
- Has the need been established?
- Is this a growing market? Is there room for your business?
- What economic, legislative and other factors have been taken into account?
- If test selling has been carried out, what has been the reaction?
- Is this a fashion or seasonal item? What will you do when business is quiet?
- What is the level of customer awareness of the product/service?
- What are the marketing objectives – sales volume, turnover, margins, number of customers? (These must be quantifiable, measurable, achievable and give time scales.)
- What is the number of sales times price required to break even?
- What is the customer profile? Are there identified clients or an order book?
- What is the level of competition? Who, where and what? What are their strengths and weaknesses? What must you do to capitalise on your strengths and to catch up where necessary?
- What is your USP? What other features and advantages can you define? Where can you 'go the extra mile'?
- What does your marketing plan consist of? Methods of advertising and promotion – what, where and when? At what cost?
- Do you have a portfolio or case studies to support your sales effort?

- What corporate image will be projected and how? (Colour, logo, name, typefaces, signage, uniforms etc.)
- What is/are the trading pattern/hours?
- What are the quality criteria and methods of measurement?
- What is the goodwill policy re complaints and service levels?
- What selling and negotiation skills are available?
- What are the terms and conditions of trading?

Suppliers

- Who and where are your suppliers?
- Why are you using them?
- Do you have a fall back in case of supplier failure?
- What are their terms and conditions?
- What stock levels will you carry and what are the controls?

Distribution

- What products will you need to distribute and how will this be done?
- What are the costs and time scales?
- Are there any security issues?

Finance

- What are the calculations for breakeven, gross and net profit?
- Is there a cashflow forecast? Does this need to cover years two and three?

- Is a profit and loss forecast included?
- How have prices been calculated? How do they compare with the competition and why are there differences?
- How have costings been calculated? Do these include your drawings (survival budget)?
- What are your personal financial objectives?
- What books are kept and by whom?
- What credit control procedures are in place?
- What funding is required and what is it for? What is your contribution and what percentage is this of the total?
- Are there other sources of funding, if so, what has been secured?
- What repayments are required and when? Does the cashflow support this?
- What security do you have and what level of risk can you accept?
- Is there a fall back plan/exit strategy in place?
- What management information is required and when? What controls are in place?

Staffing

- What numbers are required, what are their roles and what skills are required? Are the right type of staff available?
- What is the pattern for staff coverage?
- What training will they need? How, when and by whom will this be delivered and at what cost?
- How, when and at what cost will they be recruited?
- What rates will need to be paid? What are the terms and conditions and what facilities will be provided?

- What systems are in place for discipline, grievance, appraisal, motivation and development?
- How will staff need to be presented?

Premises

- What type of premises are required and where?
- What is important in terms of facilities, access, image and neighbours?
- Are the premises leased or owned? What are the terms and costs involved?
- If working from home, what resources are required and how can a working environment be created?
- Are there any issues related to image, planning or tax?

Resources

- What resources are needed in the start up phase and the future?
- What is the justification for purchase?
- What is the cost and how will they be funded/purchased?
- What is the type and value of any assets already owned?

Information Technology

- What will the system be used for i.e. tasks to be performed?
- What hardware and software will be required and how will this be supported?
- What is the level of familiarity and what training will be required?

- What security systems are in place? How will information be backed up?
- How will customers be able to contact the business?
- Will the business have a website, if so, for what purpose? Who will build this, when and at what cost? How will the site be promoted and found?

Existing businesses

- What was the start date and what has been the history?
- What is the current situation? (SWOT analysis.)
- What is the current client base? What is the size of the order book?
- Are profit and loss figures provided to cover the last three years?
- Is a balance sheet available?
- What is the level of debts receivable and ageing?

Out of the maze – appendix two

SOME SOURCES OF HELP AND INFORMATION

The following are just a few examples of the resources which are available and which have been found to be useful when starting up – it is not intended to be a definitive list. The details are correct as of April 2012. Inclusion in this list does not constitute a recommendation.

www.acas.org.uk – advice and training in regard to employment relations and human resources practice.

www.acca-business.org.uk – help with finding and choosing an accountant.

www.businesslink.gov.uk – information on many aspects of starting and running a business. See the 'starting up service' section.

www.thebfa.org – the British Franchise Association; information to help you choose a franchise.

www.barclays.co.uk – information on starting a business, plus banking services.

www.business.hsbc.co.uk – ditto.

www.lloydstsbbusiness.co.uk – ditto.

www.natwest.com – ditto.

www.rbs.co.uk – ditto.

www.companieshouse.gov.uk – guidance and information regarding forming and running a limited company.

www.britishchambers.org.uk – services and information for members of Chambers of Commerce.

www.britishlegion.org.uk – The Royal British Legion; information on the Be the Boss business start-up scheme for UK armed forces personnel.

www.direct.gov.uk – a guide to public services, all in one place.

Directory of British associations – check within your local reference library to find your representative trade or professional body.

www.dwp.gov.uk – The Department for Work and Pensions; information on jobs, benefits and pensions.

www.environment-agency.gov.uk – information and advice on the environment and waste management.

www.fsb.org.uk – The Federation of Small Businesses, providing support and services to its members; also lobbying on behalf of small businesses.

www.fpb.org – The Forum of Private Business, providing support and services to its members; also lobbying on behalf of small businesses.

www.hmrc.gov.uk – Her Majesty's Revenue and Customs; guidance on tax, National Insurance, VAT and registering a business.

www.hse.gov.uk – The Health and Safety Executive; guidance on health and safety in the workplace.

www.ico.gov.uk – The Information Commissioner's Office; guidance on compliance with the Data Protection Act.

www.ipo.gov.uk - The Intellectual Property Office; guidance on patents, trade marks, design registration and copyright.

www.lawsociety.org.uk – The Law Society's Lawyers for your Business scheme – how to access the free half hour consultation.

www.neighbourhood.statistics.gov.uk – information on your local area.

www.oft.gov.uk – The Office of Fair Trading; guidance on some of the laws that affect you when running a business.

www.payontime.co.uk – The Better Payment Practice Campaign; guidance to help you understand and exercise your rights when dealing with late payers.

www.princes-trust.org.uk– The Prince's Trust Enterprise Programme, supporting unemployed young people thinking of starting a business.

www.pcg.org.uk – PCG is the association for UK freelancers, contractors and consultants, providing guidance and services to members.

www.scavenger.net – hundreds of very readable factsheets covering many aspects of setting up and running a business, together with profiles of business opportunities. (There is a small charge for these documents.)

www.startups.co.uk – The National Federation of Enterprise Agencies; guidance on many aspects of starting up.

www.syob.co.uk – general business information and an aid to finding support in your local area.

www.tradingstandards.gov.uk – guidance on trading standards legislation, together with the Assured Trader Scheme.

Out of the maze – appendix three

GLOSSARY

Advertising. Marketing your goods or services using impersonal methods, such as newspaper advertisements or a website; often teamed with 'promotion'.

Assets. Things owned by or owed to your business, which have a monetary value; these are split into 'fixed assets' such as plant and machinery, vehicles, office equipment etc. and 'current assets' such as stock, cash in the bank and cash owed to the business. The value of any assets at a particular time is shown in the balance sheet and these figures are used to calculate any capital allowances.

Balance sheet. A document which shows an aspect of the financial position of your business by listing the assets, together with any liabilities such as money owed to your bank or suppliers; this is related to a particular point in time, usually the financial year end. In simple terms it is a statement of what your business owns and what it owes, and therefore whether it is solvent i.e. in a position to pay its debts.

Brand. The characteristics, values or image associated with a particular product or service, which influence the reputation of your business and how it is perceived by its customers. When a successful brand is created it can have a significant effect on the choices customers make and the potential for repeat business.

Breakeven. The calculation you will use to work out the sales you need to make just to cover your costs, giving you a figure where no profit or loss has been made.

Capital allowances. In addition to your day-to-day business expenses you can usually claim tax relief on capital expenditure – your fixed assets in other words; claiming this allowance will help to reduce your tax liability. The rules are complex – talk to an accountant or see www.hmrc.gov.uk for guidance.

Cashflow. An electronic or hardcopy spreadsheet, which shows the actual cash coming into and going out of your business, on a monthly and cumulative business.

Cashflow forecast. An electronic or hardcopy spreadsheet, which shows the cash which you anticipate will come into and go out of your business over the next twelve months, broken down on a monthly and cumulative basis.

Catchment area. The geographical area within which you find your customer base, often the distance you or your customers are prepared to travel. This could be local, county wide, regional, national or worldwide.

Corporate image. The way in which you present your business in the market place or the way your business is perceived by your customers.

Costing. The action of calculating the total cost of making your product, or delivering your service, in order to arrive at your cost price.

Cost price. The basic cost of making your product, or delivering your service, before adding your profit margin to arrive at your selling price. It could also be the price you charge when selling to a retailer, wholesaler or distributor, in which case it would include your profit margin - in effect it has now become your selling price.

Creditors. Suppliers or service providers to whom you owe money.

Current assets. The value of cash, stock or outstanding invoices which you could turn into cash quickly if necessary and which are likely to be realised within twelve months. These figures will appear on your balance sheet.

Current liabilities. Money which your business owes to banks, suppliers and service providers, and is due for repayment within twelve months. Again, these figures will appear on your balance sheet.

Customer base. The number and profile of customers already on your books or those you are aiming to acquire.

Customer profile. The type(s) of customers already on your books or those you are aiming to acquire, defined by such factors as age, sex, location, spending power, whether business or private etc.

Debtors. Persons or businesses to whom/to which you owe money.

Depreciation. The drop in the value of a fixed asset on a year on year basis; this figure will be shown as an expense on your profit and loss statement, thus reducing your profit and therefore your tax liability.

Desk research. Market research you carry out using data collected by others, such as directories and government or local authority statistics. Obvious sources are libraries and the internet.

Direct costs. The cost of materials and labour involved in the production of goods or the delivery of services, also known as variable costs. These will vary month by month, as a result of increases or decreases in production and sales.

Drawings. The term for the money you take out of your business as income when you trade as a sole trader or partner; your drawings are not an allowable business expense.

Expenses. The price of goods or services which you incur as part of running your business, not including the purchase of fixed assets. Most of these are likely to be allowable, that is, offset against the value of your sales thus reducing your profits and your tax liability. To be allowable, expenses must be wholly and exclusively incurred in pursuit of your business and be properly recorded; for guidance talk to an accountant or see www.hmrc.gov.uk.

Elevator pitch. A very short summary of your business idea, covering who you are, what you do and what makes your business special. This can be extremely useful when networking.

FAB An acronym standing for feature, advantage and benefit, all of which terms are used in the selling process. A feature can be defined as something which is integral to a product or service, such as size, colour, power output or facilities provided. An advantage is then what a particular feature could do for a customer, such as save time, money or inconvenience; advantages are general, being applicable to any potential customer. When it comes to selling, features and advantages are the basis of your product knowledge, however to be successful you will have to establish a customer's needs; the benefit only comes into play when you have shown that your product or service meets those needs.

Field research. This is the collection of new or additional market research information, which you (or your researchers) have carried out using surveys and/or observation. This will usually be more relevant to your business and up-to-date than your desk research.

Fixed assets. Assets owned by your business (such as plant and machinery) intended for long term use and which are depreciated over a period of years.

Fixed costs. Business expenses that remain at the same level, irrespective of the amount of your sales, such as rent, business rates and insurance. These bills have to be paid even if you make no sales at all. They are also known as standing costs.

Franchise. A form of trading where you buy into a proven business concept; you are self-employed and usually have a defined trading territory, but are bound by the terms of your contract with your franchisor and work within the guidelines set out in their business model.

Gross profit. This figure is your total income from sales, minus your direct costs; you still have to deduct your day-to-day expenses from this figure to arrive at your net profit.

Gross profit percentage/margin. This is your gross profit figure in pounds, expressed as a percentage of your sales. To calculate this figure, divide your gross profit by your sales and multiply by 100 e.g. gross profit £8, sales £12 = 66% gross profit margin.

Indirect costs. Another term for your day-to-day expenses.

Insolvency. The situation which would arise if your business could not pay its debts, even if you sold all the assets.

Intellectual property. The term which covers patents, trade mark and design registration and copyright; these forms of protection help to prevent others from benefitting from your inventiveness and creativity. Your intellectual property could have considerable value, such as the royalties on music you have written.

Lease. This is a legal document in which a landlord gives you the right to occupy their premises for a fixed period in return for the payment of rent. Leasing is also a way of acquiring assets without paying for them outright; in effect, you are hiring them and do not own them.

Legal status. This is the form of business you have adopted when you start to trade e.g. sole trader, partnership, limited company, limited liability partnership or social enterprise.

Liabilities. The money which you owe to your bank, suppliers or service providers.

Limited company. A form of trading where the finances of the business are separate from yours, the main advantage being that your financial liability is limited to the value of the shares when the company was set up. The company is a separate legal entity, registered at Companies House. You will be on the payroll and therefore subject to tax and NI at source.

Limited liability partnership. A variation on the normal partnership, in that your financial liability is limited to the amount of money you have put into the business; you will still take drawings rather than be on the payroll, but the partnership will be registered at Companies House, making it more complex to set up and run than an ordinary partnership.

Margins. Your gross and net profit expressed as a percentage of your sales.

Market share. The 'slice' of the available market that you have acquired or plan to acquire. It can be expressed as a percentage of the total market/sales, by the number of customers making up your customer base, or in pounds.

Marketing plan. A crucial part of your business plan and ongoing planning; this is the document which sets out the ways in which you will advertise and promote your business, who is responsible for each action, together with timings, deadlines and costs. As usual, these costs will appear in your cashflow.

Mark up. The amount by which you have increased the cost price of a bought in product or service to arrive at your selling price. For example, if the cost price to you is £10 and you sell the item for £20, you will have marked it up by £10 or 100%.

Net profit. This figure is your income from sales, minus your direct costs and all other business expenses. If you trade as a limited company, your salary will be shown as an expense of the business; however, if you trade as a sole trader or partner, the net profit figure will be the basis of your tax bill as your drawings are not an allowable expense and the Inland Revenue assumes that all the profits that the business has made have come to you.

Net profit percentage/margin. This is your net profit in pounds expressed as a percentage of your sales; to calculate this divide your net profit by your sales and multiply by 100 e.g. net profit £3, sales £12 = 25% net profit margin.

Niche. You cannot please all of the people all of the time; this means that you should concentrate your marketing effort on those customers who are most likely to buy your product or service and on any gap in the market where you believe you can compete most effectively. In other words, you are carving out a 'niche'.

Order book. The business you have on hand – orders for goods and/or bookings in your diary for services which have been contracted.

Outsourcing. Using outside providers to help you run your business, such as accountants, bookkeepers, secretarial services etc. This can often be more cost effective than doing it yourself, especially where you lack knowledge or confidence.

Overheads. Another word for your day-to-day expenses, not including your direct costs.

Partnership. Two or more people forming a business and sharing the responsibilities, risks and rewards. The partners are self-employed and have 'joint and several liability', which means that their personal assets could be seized to pay off any business debts.

Pre-start expenses. These are the expenses which you might incur before you start trading; as long as these are necessary to enable you to start your business (and are properly documented), they should be allowable and therefore reduce your tax liability when your first year accounts are prepared.

Product knowledge. This is all the information related to the features and advantages of your product or service, together with things like your terms and conditions, which you will rely on to make a convincing sales pitch to your customers. In short, 'you must know what you are talking about'.

Profit. The surplus of income over expenditure; in effect, your net profit.

Profit and loss. A statement produced at the end of your financial year (or more often if desired), showing your sales income for the year and your spending, broken down by category of expense, thus allowing the calculation of your gross and net profit or loss. This is then used in the preparation of your tax return.

Profit and loss forecast. An electronic or hardcopy spreadsheet which shows the estimated profit and loss for your business for the next trading year, usually teamed up with your cashflow forecast. Ideally, this would show monthly figures as well as the total for the year.

Promotion. Marketing your goods or services using more interpersonal methods, such as networking, social networking, writing articles, seeking press coverage and using word-of-mouth referrals to target customers. Often teamed up with advertising as in 'advertising and promotion'.

Repeat business. The same customers coming back you on a regular basis, usually achieved by providing a level of service which consistently exceeds their expectations, thus building a solid reputation. Keeping the customers you have is more cost effective than having to find new ones.

Route to market. The way in which you gain access to your customers, such as your website, shop, wholesaler or market stall.

Running costs. Another term for the day-to-day expenses incurred as a result of operating your business.

Salary. The money you pay yourself (i.e. wages) when trading as a limited company, which will be subject to PAYE.

Sales. The income your business derives from selling products or services; also known as turnover.

Sales volume. The number of products or services you sell in a given period of time.

Selling price. The price you charge your customers for your product or service, which not only covers your costs but leaves you with a profit.

Social enterprise. A business with a social purpose, such as keeping a village shop open for the benefit of the community; any profits are used for that purpose and are not taken by shareholders or managers.

Sole trader. The simplest form of business status; you are self-employed and you and your business are seen as being one and the same. You are personally liable for any business debts and take your income in the form of drawings.

Standing costs. These are your bills which have to be paid, irrespective of the sales income you generate; for example rent, rates, insurance, power etc.

Survival budget. The amount of money you must take out of your business in the form of salary or drawings, in order to pay your personal bills and to maintain your lifestyle.

SWOT analysis. An acronym standing for 'strengths, weaknesses, opportunities and threats.' Analysing where your business stands by looking in detail at each of these four headings.

Target market. The group, or groups, of private customers or businesses that you focus on, when marketing your product or service.

Terms and conditions. The guidelines or provisions covering the way in which you do business with your customers or your suppliers do business with you; these will deal with such topics as the timing of payments, limits of liability, ownership of goods, action in the case of late or non-payment etc.

Turnover. The income that your business derives from selling products, or services, also known as sales.

USP. An acronym for your unique selling point, which is the aspect of you, your product or service which really makes you and your business stand out from your competition and which you will try to put across in all of your advertising and promotion.

Variable costs. These are the costs which will increase or decrease in line with your productivity and sales, such as materials and labour; also known as direct costs.

Viability. Your business becomes viable when, based on your research and planning, it can be shown that it can pay its way and has a good chance of being profitable in the long term.

Virtual office. The situation where you do not occupy actual office space, but do have some outsourced secretarial backup and a business address; this can make you appear more professional and ensure that all your telephone calls are answered. This service is usually available from serviced office providers.

Working capital. This is the value of your current assets, minus your current liabilities.

Year end. The date your accounts are made up to, usually but not necessarily, twelve months from your start date; another topic to discuss with an accountant.

Out of the maze – appendix four

YOUR BUSINESS STATUS – SOME PLUSES AND MINUSES

Sole trader.

<u>Some pluses.</u>

Very simple to set up.

You are the business – there is no separate legal entity.

Your accounts and tax returns can be kept simple.

Your financial records are not in the public domain.

You have the option of changing your business status at a later date.

It is easy to wind up the business.

<u>Some minuses.</u>

You are personally liable for any business debts – you could lose everything.

It can be more difficult to raise funds or to sell your business.

You can feel isolated unless you have a support team and/or network.

You may be entitled to fewer social security benefits.

Partnership.

<u>Some pluses</u> – similar to sole trader status, but in addition:

You have more support.

You may be able to call on more in the way of funds, skills, knowledge and contacts.

<u>Some minuses.</u>

Each partner is liable for <u>all</u> the debts of the business.

It is wise to have a partnership agreement in place, to avoid any disputes.

You are sharing the decision making – therefore you have less control.

Limited liability partnership.

<u>A plus.</u>

You are protected to some extent from the liabilities of the business.

<u>A minus.</u>

The partnership needs to be registered at Companies House and accounts must be filed there. Some of this information will be in the public domain and reporting is more complex.

Limited company.

<u>Some pluses.</u>

Your business may have greater credibility with customers and suppliers.

Your liability for any business debts is reduced – the company is a separate legal entity.

It can be easier to raise finance.

There can be tax advantages.

<u>Some minuses.</u>

There is more complexity and 'red tape'.

Your accountant's fees are likely to be higher.

You are on PAYE – someone must run the payroll.

Your business will pay Employers National Insurance on your behalf.

It is more difficult to wind up the business.

Much of your financial information will be in the public domain.

You may be asked to personally guarantee any borrowing.

Note: These are just some of the points you might consider before deciding on your business status; if you are in any doubt as to what is best for you and your business, then talk to an accountant or solicitor.

Out of the maze – appendix five

POSSIBLE TASKS WHEN RUNNING YOUR BUSINESS

Task	Yes	No
Planning and control, day-to-day and long term		
Setting and monitoring standards		
Preparing accounts and tax returns		
Bookkeeping		
PAYE		
Invoicing, credit control and chasing debts		
Paying the bills		
Costing and pricing		
Preparing and monitoring the cashflow		
Calculating and monitoring breakeven and profit margins		
Market research, preparing and actioning the marketing plan		
Advertising, promotion and public relations		
Selling and negotiating		

Handling sales enquiries		
Dealing with problems and complaints		
Stock control and ordering		
Staff recruitment and training		
Staff management, motivation and discipline		
Complying with legislation		
Security		
Arranging and maintaining insurances		
The website and IT		
Production. Packaging and delivery		
Health and safety		
Maintenance of equipment and property		
Networking		

Tick the 'yes' or 'no' box to indicate whether a particular task is relevant to you and your business model. This is not an exhaustive list – there may be other tasks which you will have to carry out; if there is more than one person in the management team, decide who is responsible for a particular task.

Out of the maze – appendix six

SOME EXAMPLES OF PERSONALITY TRAITS

The following are some aspects of personality which could be helpful when running a business; which of these could you 'bring to the party'?

Trait	Yes	No
You enjoy and respond to a challenge		
You are clear about what your business offers and what makes it special		
You are prepared to put in the effort and the hours		
You can weigh up the risks and make decisions		
You enjoy the work you are doing and relate to your customers		
You have clear goals and a strategy to achieve them		
You are comfortable with working in isolation		
You are comfortable with responsibility		
You can cope with the lack of security		
You can cope with reversals of fortune		

You are methodical and consistent in your approach		
You are a doer as well as a thinker		
You see the glass as being half full rather than half empty		
You have confidence in your abilities		
You are not too proud to ask for help and to listen to advice		
You look like and behave as a professional		
You can talk easily and confidently to people you do not know		
You are a good listener		
You have both physical and mental stamina		
You have backing from your family		
You are prepared to make sacrifices		
You understand your limitations		
You are good at multitasking		
You have a good memory or always write things down		
You do not take complaints or criticism personally		

You are a 'people person'		

Out of the maze – appendix seven

SOME EXAMPLES OF BUSINESS RELATED SKILLS

The following are some of the skills which could be helpful when running your business – which do you possess?

The maths	Yes	No
You are good with figures		
You can draft a cashflow forecast		
You can draft a profit and loss forecast		
You can calculate your profit margins and breakeven		
You can accurately cost your product or service		
You can keep proper books		
You can operate a credit control system		
You can run a payroll		

The market	Yes	No
You can negotiate in order to obtain the best price		
You can state the features and advantages of		

	Yes	No
your product or service		
You can focus on and convey your USP		
You can close a sale		
You can communicate fluently and professionally, both orally and in writing		
You can write your own copy for your advertising or website		
You can create a practical and effective marketing plan		
You can carry out meaningful market research		
You can relate to your customers, no matter what their status or background		
You can network effectively		

The people	Yes	No
You can identify and recruit suitable staff		
You can train, motivate and discipline staff		
You can set an example to your staff		
You understand and can comply with employment law		

You can plan to obtain the most effective staff coverage		

Running the show	Yes	No
You finish what you start		
You use your time effectively		
You can make a decision, having weighed up the options		
You can deal with any 'red tape'		
You can use your computer hardware and software effectively		
You understand your accountant, solicitor or account manager		
You take advice and act on it		
You can apply high standards to your own performance and be self-critical		
You respond positively to problems and complaints and follow them through to a satisfactory resolution		

No one will have all these skills, but try to identify those you have; be honest and objective. Use these to sell yourself to the reader and to give you confidence in your own abilities.

Out of the maze – appendix eight

SOURCES FOR MARKET RESEARCH

The following are just some of the resources you can tap into to find the information you need, in order to answer the questions contained in the business plan. Firstly decide which questions you need to answer; secondly decide on the best place to look for the information you need; thirdly – start your research!

- Your accountant.
- Your bank.
- Business books.
- Business directories.
- Business support organisations.
- Competition – their websites and publicity material, talking to their customers or posing as a customer.
- The census.
- Desk research – what information is out there already?
- Feedback from your customers.
- Field research – getting out and about.
- The internet – see 'Appendix Two - Sources of help and information' for some of the useful sites to be found.
- Local government websites and economic development units.
- Local, county and national newspapers.
- Magazines – national, local, trade and special interest.
- Market research companies.

- Networking.
- Your records, audits, complaints and problems.
- Reference libraries.
- Your solicitor.
- Your suppliers.
- Surveys and questionnaires, carried out face-to-face, over the telephone, by e mail or on paper.
- Tourism bodies.
- TV and radio news and business programmes.
- Trade fairs and seminars.
- Trade and professional bodies.

Out of the maze – appendix nine

THE CASHFLOW FORECAST

To begin with there are some principles or guidelines which you should bear in mind when creating your cashflow forecast; these are reflected in the example exercise.

- The cashflow is 'time sensitive'; this means that when you enter the figures for any money coming into your business into the cashflow, you will enter them in the column for the month when the money will reach your bank account and not in the column for the month when you do the work or raise the invoice. Similarly, any money going out of your business is shown in the month when you pay the bill and not in the month when you order or receive the goods or services.

- The term 'cash' covers any payment you receive at the time you make the sale; the term 'credit sales' (or 'debtors') covers any payment you receive having raised an invoice and awaited payment.

- The term 'opening bank balance' relates to any cash balance in your bank account, carried over from the end of one month to the start of the next month. If you are just starting to trade there will be no opening bank balance in month one – there is nothing to carry forward.

- Your 'closing bank balance' shows how much cash you have to work with, both on a monthly and cumulative basis. To arrive at this figure you take your total income from all sources, subtract your total payments to arrive at your surplus or deficit figure for the month, then add or subtract your opening bank balance. This final figure is your closing bank balance, which in turn becomes your opening bank balance for the following month.

- It is wise to start your cashflow in the month when you begin to spend money in preparation to be able to trade, rather than starting in the month when you actually start trading. For example, you plan to start trading in September, but have to spend money in July and August; this approach will give you a truer picture of the state of your finances.

- When you are setting out your forecast figures, all of these sums will be entered in the 'forecast' column, rather than the 'actual' column, even if you know the cost to the penny. You should only complete the actual column at the month end when you do your books.

- Do not make life difficult for yourself when forecasting – don't bother with pence or pound signs, round your figures to the nearest pound. A cashflow forecast will never be exact, all you can do is to try to be as accurate as possible with the information you have. This approach also avoids clutter.

- The cashflow will always include VAT, whether you are VAT registered or not; you will pay VAT on your purchases and will pass this cost on in your pricing. (If you are not VAT registered you will use the price to you, inclusive of VAT, as the starting point for your costing and pricing calculations.) If you are VAT registered you will need to calculate the amount of VAT you will pay on a quarterly basis and include these figures in your cashflow.

- Your cashflow should reflect the build-up in sales and the seasonality of your business; your income will vary month to month, according to your busy and quieter periods of trading.
- If you are a sole trader or partner, you will show your drawings as a separate item to any wages you pay your staff; if you run a limited company, you will include your salary in the company wage bill.
- If you pay for anything outright, you will enter this as a one-off payment in the month the bill is paid; if you pay for anything on a monthly or quarterly basis, then you will show these purchases broken down as monthly or quarterly payments.

The cashflow exercise.

There are three sheets provided for this: firstly, a blank cashflow for you to complete using the information given below; secondly, an 'answer sheet' – the completed cashflow to enable you to check your figures. Thirdly, another blank cashflow for you to use when creating your own cashflow forecast when you are ready to do this. Please bear in mind that there is no standard cashflow format; there may be some expenses you will incur that do not appear within the example – likewise, there may be some expenses which you will not incur. You can alter your cashflow to suit your business circumstances.

The following is the information you will need to complete the exercise.

- Your situation: you are a sole trader, employing one member of staff. You will be VAT registered as your turnover will exceed the current VAT threshold. You plan to start trading in September, ready for the Christmas trade.

- You open a business bank account in July and deposit £6,000 of your own money into this account. You have also negotiated a £2,000 overdraft facility.

- You buy a new computer in July, which costs £790.

- In August you buy a second hand van for £3,650; road tax is £230, insurance costs £425. You pay all of these bills in full. You also take out public and product liability insurance in August, together with employer's liability insurance – the total cost is £48 per month, paid by direct debit. You have your business cards printed at a cost of £80, paid for in full.

- You take on an employee in August, in order to complete his/her training; the wage bill, including Employers National Insurance, works out at £1,700 per month gross.

- You make your first sales in September; where possible you ask for payment by cash or cheque. However, most customers insist on an invoice and trade terms – you allow thirty days to pay. Cash sales over the next ten months are projected to be £1800, £1600, £2100, £1400, £1900, £2400, £1800, £1250, £1700 and £1300 respectively. Credit sales invoiced over the next ten months are projected to be £4700, £7200, £5600, £4900, £7600, £8400, £7800, £9000, £8300 and £8100 respectively. It is expected that customers will pay on time.

- The cost of any material used is calculated to be 40% of the value of the sale; you have negotiated thirty day terms of payment with your trade suppliers.

- You rent a lock-up unit in September; rent and rates are £750 per quarter, paid in advance. Gas and electricity will cost £45 per month, paid by direct debit.

- You plan to have a brochure printed in November at a cost of £480; you have thirty days to pay the invoice.

- The cost of your telephone and broadband is projected to be £37 per month once you start trading, paid by direct debit.

- You plan to advertise monthly in two local magazines at a cost of £220 per month, starting in August; you have thirty days to pay the invoice.

- You calculate the average monthly cost of diesel for your van as £240, once you start trading in earnest. You put this cost on a credit card, which will be paid off in full during the following month. You will also have to replace the tyres at a cost of £180, probably in February.

- You have an accountant who will charge £700 per annum to prepare your profit and loss and to file your tax return; however, he will not invoice for this work until he has completed your first years figures.

- You plan to take £1,800 per month in drawings, starting in October, and from which you will pay your tax and national insurance.

- As you are VAT registered there is likely to be a payment to be made each quarter; this payment will be the difference between the VAT you have charged and the VAT you have paid and is due within a month of the quarter end. To calculate the VAT contained in a gross figure at the current rate of VAT (20%) – simply divide the gross by six.

Please note: for the purposes of this exercise it has been assumed that VAT is payable on all bills for products or services, although in real life this may not always be the case. Of course, there is no VAT included in the figures for PAYE or drawings

CASHFLOW EXERCISE – EXPLANATORY NOTES

- As a sole trader you will take drawings while your staff will be on PAYE.

- Your £6000 investment in your business, will be shown as 'Own cash introduced', going into your account in July. The overdraft figure is not shown as this is simply a facility provided by your bank and is not actual cash.

- Your computer will be a 'capital purchase' in July.

- Your van is also a 'capital purchase' shown as a one-off payment in August; the road tax and insurance is paid in full at the same time.

- Your other forms of insurance come into force in August and are paid for on a monthly basis.

- As stated, your employee's wages are shown as 'PAYE', starting in August.

- Your cash sales are shown in the month during which they take place; however, your credit sales are shown in the month following, as customers will pay in arrears.

- Your material costs are simply 40% of your sales; the payments are delayed until the next month following the sales they are related to, as you will be taking advantage of your trade terms. However, although the bills are paid in arrears they are based on the total value of the sales made in the previous month i.e. both paid in cash and invoiced.

- Your rent and rates are paid at the beginning of each quarter, starting in September; your gas and electricity bills are shown under 'heat, light and power'.

- The bill for your brochure will be paid in December, taking advantage of your thirty days credit.

- Your telephone and broadband bill is paid during the month in which it occurs.

- Your first invoice for advertising will be paid in September, again taking advantage of your thirty days credit.

- Your first bill for diesel will be paid in October, when you settle your credit card bill; the cost of new tyres is included in the February column although it could be incurred sooner or later – the point is that you have made provision for this cost.

- You will not receive a bill from the accountant until year two, once your first year accounts have been reconciled.

- Your drawings are shown as 'proprietor's drawings', starting in October.

- Your first VAT quarter will run from September to November, with your first payment due in December; this quarter might also include any VAT paid prior to starting up – for instance on the capital and other purchases made in July and August, as in this example.

The following figures may be helpful in explaining how the VAT payments were calculated:

Quarter	Sales	VAT	Expenses	VAT	Difference
September/November	17,400	2,900	13,623	2,270	630
December/February	23,800	3,966	12,580	2,097	1,869
March/ May	29,950	4,992	14,780	2,463	2,529

- In order to avoid confusion, it is helpful to place brackets around any figures which indicate a minus figure.

You will see from the cashflow example that there is no margin for error where this business is concerned, as it appears to be leading a 'hand to mouth' existence, running a deficit for most of the time and in some months significantly exceeding its overdraft limit. If your actual cashflow were to develop along these lines, you would need to look for ways to increase turnover, to speed up customer payments and to cut your costs where possible; this could include reducing your drawings until such time as the business finances are strong enough to allow you to increase them once more. You can also see that your cashflow forecast enables you to plan, to take decisions and not least, to establish the viability of your business.

Out of the maze – appendix ten

REASONS TO BUY

Customers don't buy your product or service, they buy what it does for them; the following are some of the words or phrases you might use in your advertising or promotion in order to get your message across:

Saves time	Saves money	Value for money	Accessible
User friendly	Jargon free	Quality	Substantial
Professional	Fun	Colourful	Ethical
New	Acclaimed	Cost effective	Timely
Flexible	Local	Practical	Confidence
Quick	National	Mobile	Satisfying
Efficient	International	Established	Personal touch
Reliable	Logical	Durable	Ongoing support
Unique	Value added	Ideal	Experienced
Bespoke	Beneficial	While-you-wait	Knowledgeable
Tailored	Environmentall	One stop	Well being

	y friendly	shop	
Specialist	Fair trade	Discreet	Modern
Customer focussed	Safe	Handmade	Classic
Customer led	Innovative	British made	Clean
Hi-tech	Ground breaking	Guaranteed	Healthy
Reputable	Tested	Exact	Independent
Comfortable	Traditional		

Which of these words describes you and/or your business? Stating your qualifications, membership of a trade or professional body or approved supplier status could also be helpful in encouraging customers to buy your product or service and to come back to you.

Out of the maze – appendix eleven

SURVIVAL BUDGET

How much do you need to take out of your business, as salary or drawings, in order to pay your personal bills and to maintain your lifestyle? Draw up a list of all the things you spend money on, on a weekly, monthly or annual frequency – refer to your bank and credit card statements and utility bills for this information. Then total your annual spend for each of these expenses. Add up this last column to indicate the minimum amount you must take as income during the year; don't forget this figure will be net, after you have paid tax and National Insurance. Therefore, the actual amount you take out of the business is likely to be considerably higher.

Expense	Average weekly spend	Average monthly spend	Annual total
Mortgage/rent			
Council tax			
Gas and electricity			
Water rates			
Food			
Other household			
Insurances			
Savings/pension			

Telephone/broadband			
Subscriptions			
Clothes, shoes etc.			
Holidays			
Entertainment			
TV licence			
Loan payments			
Car tax and insurance			
Car running costs			
Living expenses			
Presents/Christmas			
Other			
Other			
Total for the year			

Having calculated your total for the year, enter the tax inclusive figure into your cashflow under the heading of salary or drawings, whichever is applicable.

Out of the maze – appendix twelve

PROFILING YOUR CUSTOMERS

The following are some of the ways in which you can start to define the profile of your customers, in order to target them more effectively.

Firstly – the man or woman in the street.

- By their motivation to buy – needs or desires.
- By their age, sex and occupation.
- By their social class.
- By where they live and the type of property they occupy.
- By their income and spending power.
- By what they read, watch and listen to.
- By the means of transport they use.
- By where they go and what they do for entertainment.
- By their marital and family status.
- By their religion or politics.
- By their education and qualifications.
- By their culture and ethnicity.
- By who makes the decisions.
- By their shopping habits and how often they buy.
- By their brand loyalty or lack of it.

Secondly – when you are dealing with businesses.

- By the opportunities they have, now and in the future.
- By the problems they face, now and in the future.

- By the geographical area within which they trade.
- By their location and where buying decisions are made.
- By their customer base and the needs of their customers.
- By their size and spending power.
- By the publications that are read and the trade fairs attended.
- By whether they are a new or established business.
- By whether they are high or low tech.
- By their reputation and share of the market.
- By whether they are in a service, manufacturing or retail environment.
- By the language and/or jargon used.
- By how they prefer to be approached and the networks used.

Out of the maze – appendix thirteen

SOME CUSTOMER PROFILE EXAMPLES

A profile of your target private customer could look something like this:

'Male or female, between thirty and fifty years of age; educated to degree level, at management level holding down a demanding job. Earns an above average income but has a limited disposable income. Lives within a thirty mile radius in a rural location or an up-market area of town. Prefers to shop on-line rather than locally. In long term relationship, with children at school or in higher education. Uses own transport rather than public transport unless travelling long distances. Reads a broadsheet newspaper and quality special interest or fashion magazines; listens to BBC Radio Four and has a digital television subscription. Wide network of friends and participates in varied social activities; uses social networking sites. Expects a rapid response and consistent quality of service, which is more important than price.'

A profile of your target business customer could look something like this:

'Construction firms located within a forty mile radius, specialising in domestic repairs and extensions rather than new builds. Owner managed with a small number of staff, turnover in excess of 200K. Lacking time to organise, manage or market effectively; dependent on local reputation for obtaining work. Unable to keep up with developments in their industry. Reads trade magazines and belongs to a trade body; not registered on any approved supplier networks. Opportunity to cost effectively outsource day-to-day administration and to update image; also to improve profit margins by use of up-to-date techniques and materials.'

Having completed your customer profile(s) ask yourself what openings there may be to sell your product or service in response to your target customers' opportunities or problems and the needs or desires which you have identified; also what methods of advertising and promotion would be most likely to be effective with a particular customer group?

Out of the maze – appendix fourteen

IDENTIFYING COMPETITORS

The following are some of the resources which might help you to identify your competition.

Two obvious ones to start with:

The internet – search by category of business, by location and by individual website. Use on line directories e.g. www.scoot.co.uk, www.thomsonlocal.com, www.yell.com.

Reference libraries – business directories and telephone directories. Ask the staff for help with your research – what other resources in the form of databases and reports can they tap into on your behalf?

Then:

- Chambers of commerce.
- Companies House.
- Field research e.g. local trading estates and high streets.
- Local government publications or websites.
- Local radio.
- Local, regional and national newspapers, including free papers.
- Market research companies.
- Networking.
- Specialist trade, professional or general interest magazines.
- Trade fairs and seminars.

- Trade and professional bodies – lists of members.

Please note: it is likely that you will have to become a member of a Chamber or a trade or professional body in order to gain access to a list of members.

Out of the maze – appendix fifteen

COSTING EXAMPLES

To make a profit you must obviously charge more for your product or service than it costs to make or deliver. There is no point in selling a product or service which is not profitable – you would be working for no return; hence the importance of calculating an accurate cost price.

Although the associated terminology is covered in the glossary, it is worth repeating here; confusingly there are various terms for the same type of costs. Firstly there are 'direct' costs, also known as 'variables'; as you will guess from the title, these will vary in direct proportion to your productivity and sales. When you are busy they will increase, when business is slack they will reduce. These terms generally cover the materials used in a production process, together with the cost of any labour involved in the production of goods or the delivery of a service. *(See appendix sixteen – breakeven and profit margins and appendix seventeen – profit and loss forecast, for examples as to how these costs are broken down and shown.)*

Secondly, there are 'overheads' also known as 'indirect' or 'running' costs; these are all the other bills incurred in the running of your business, some of which are described as 'fixed'. This last category includes such things as rent, rates, water, power and insurance – these bills have to be paid whatever the level of sales.

There are a number of ways in which you could calculate the cost of producing your product or delivering your service, giving you a reasonably accurate figure at the outset, which can be revisited once you start trading and produce actual figures. Here are three of them.

The first is also covered in the section on finance; it is based on the premise that each sale will make a contribution towards the cost of any materials and labour (directs), and your overheads, drawings or salary (gross, before tax). Don't forget that if you are not VAT registered and therefore cannot offset any VAT you pay on your purchases, you will have to use the VAT inclusive price you have paid as your starting point in the calculation and thus pass on this cost in turn to your customers. You will need to calculate these costs with the help of your cashflow forecast, also the number of sales you expect to make during the year. For example, if your direct cost for materials used comes to £18,000, your overheads total £13,500 and your drawings are planned to be £28,000, with a target of 250 sales during the year, then the figures would look like this:

Direct costs   £18,000 ÷ 250 = £72

Overheads   £13,500 ÷ 250 = £54

Drawings   £28,000 ÷ 250 = £112

Cost price   = £238

To this figure you would need to add your desired profit margin to arrive at your selling price, which must be a price which your customers are prepared to pay.

If you are selling a service i.e. selling your time, you can take a different approach. To begin with you will need to calculate the number of weeks you can, or want to work during the year, allowing for holidays, downtime due to sickness or training and/or the availability of customers. Then you will need to estimate the number of hours you will invoice on average during each of these weeks; you may *work* a forty five hour week, but only be able to *invoice* for thirty two hours, the rest being used for research or administration. This approach allows you to calculate your cost per hour to cover your overheads and salary or drawings and thus work out an hourly and daily rate. For example:

Average number of weeks to be worked
    47

Average number of hours to be invoiced per week
    32

Number of hours to be invoiced in total   47 x 32 =
1504

Cost of overheads
    £13,500

Hourly charge to cover overheads   13,500 ÷ 1504 =
£8.98

Drawings
£28,000

Hourly charge to cover drawings   28000 ÷ 1504 =
£18.61

Total hourly charge to cover costs
£27.59

You would add your desired profit margin to this figure to arrive at your selling price per hour and your daily rate; if there were any material or labour costs involved in the delivery of your service, these would need to be added to the hourly rate before setting your selling price.

Another option is available if you are manufacturing a product; the cost of the item will be your direct costs of materials and labour, plus the share of your overheads that the item should carry i.e. every item you produce must carry its fair share. Therefore you will need to calculate the percentage of your sales that a specific product is likely to contribute to arrive at your 'fair share' figure.

For example: you manufacture five products, one of which is expected to contribute 20% of your sales; if your overheads are £13,500 then the contribution would be £2,700. If you plan to make and sell 600 of this product, then each one will contribute £4.50 towards your overheads; to this figure you would add the cost of the materials used in the manufacturing process (including any wastage), together with the cost of labour. This will involve detailed research and trial production runs to obtain accurate figures.

The final calculation might look like this:

Contribution to overheads	£4.50
Materials – total cost of components	£6.15
Labour – 2 hours @ £8.20 per hour	£16.40
Total cost per item	£27.05

As always, you would need to add your desired profit margin to this figure.

As has been stated, calculating your costs accurately is really important if your business is to grow while providing you with the income you need; if in doubt, seek help with your calculations from an accountant, business adviser or mentor.

Out of the maze – appendix sixteen

BREAKEVEN AND PROFIT MARGINS EXERCISE

The calculations for breakeven and gross and net profit are some of the ratios which can be used to measure the financial performance of your business; they can help you to assess the health of your business as well as enabling you to take decisions based on facts, and to take remedial action if necessary.

Gross profit margin.

This figure shows the percentage contribution earned on each £ of sales, after deducting your direct costs, usually materials and labour. Businesses that use materials or stock will need to carry out a stocktake to work out these direct costs (or cost of sales); this involves counting any opening stock, adding purchases made during the year and subtracting any closing stock.

The equation you use to calculate your gross profit margin (or percentage) is: gross profit in pounds, divided by sales in pounds, multiplied by one hundred. For example, if your sales were £42,000, with £29,000 gross profit after deducting your direct costs of £13,000, then your gross profit margin would be $29,000 \div 42,000 \times 100 = 69\%$.

Breakeven.

You will need your gross profit margin in order to calculate your breakeven figure; the equation you use is: your overheads, divided by your gross profit margin, multiplied by one hundred. For example, if your overheads were £16,000 and your gross profit margin was 69%, then your breakeven figure would be 16000 ÷ 69% x 100 = 23,188.

Net profit margin.

This figure shows the percentage contribution earned on each £ of sales after deducting all your costs. (Note: if you are a sole trader or partner your net profit figure in pounds will be shown on your profit and loss statement as 'net profit before drawings' and will be the starting point for calculating the amount of your tax liability – this figure must also more than cover your survival budget.) The equation you use to calculate your net profit margin is: net profit in pounds, divided by sales in pounds, multiplied by one hundred. For example, if your sales were £42,000, and your total costs were £29,000, giving a net profit in pounds of £13,000, then your net profit margin would be 13,000 ÷ 42,000 x 100 = 30.9%.

Increase or decreases in your gross and net profit margins will tell you whether you are becoming more or less efficient in generating profit; it is easier to spot a trend if you are using percentage figures rather than pounds. You can calculate your margins annually; however, it is much better if you calculate them monthly; if there is a problem you will discover it sooner rather than later and can take remedial action.

Exercise.

Using the figures contained in the cashflow exercise, now try calculating the gross profit, breakeven and net profit examples contained in the financial projection sheets. Remember, when calculating profit you will need to count all the sales *generated* in the trading year, together with all the costs *incurred* in the trading year, irrespective of whether you have been paid by your customers or have paid your bills.

Sheet one is a blank sheet for you to complete, sheet two is the answer sheet, while sheet three is for the profit and breakeven calculations which you will include in your business plan. There are also notes to explain how the exercise figures were arrived at. Please note: to avoid unnecessary complication, please assume for the purpose of this exercise that you are not VAT registered and therefore all the figures will be gross figures.

Out of the maze – appendix sixteen

BREAKEVEN AND PROFIT MARGINS: SHEET ONE – BLANK

First calculate your gross profit for the year:

Projected sales		£
Minus direct costs: Materials Labour		£ £
Total direct costs		£
Gross profit in pounds		£

Calculate your gross profit margin – your gross profit in pounds, divided by your sales in pounds, times one hundred. Gross profit margin =   %

Calculate your overheads for the year, prior to calculating your breakeven figure.

Heat, light and power	£
Printing and stationery	£
Insurance	£
Telephone and broadband	£

Advertising and promotion	£
Van	£
Professional fees	£
Rent	£
Other	£
Loan payments	£
Total overheads	£

Calculate the sales you need, in order to break even – your overheads in pounds, divided by your gross profit margin, times one hundred. Breakeven figure = £

Divide this figure by twelve, to calculate your monthly breakeven figure.

Monthly breakeven figure = £

Calculate your net profit for the year in pounds, together with your net profit margin.

Projected sales	£
Minus breakeven figure	£
Balance	£
Multiply by gross profit margin (%)	
Net profit in pounds	£

Divide the net profit by your sales and multiply by one hundred	
Net profit margin =	%

Out of the maze – appendix sixteen

BREAKEVEN AND PROFIT MARGINS: SHEET TWO – ANSWERS

First calculate your gross profit for the year:

Projected sales		£88,850
Minus direct costs:		
Materials		£35,540
Labour		£18,700
Total direct costs		£54,240
Gross profit in pounds		£34,610

Calculate your gross profit margin – your gross profit in pounds, divided by your sales in pounds, times one hundred. Gross profit margin = 38.9%

Calculate your overheads for the year, prior to calculating your breakeven figure.

Heat, light and power	£450
Printing and stationery	£560
Insurance	£528
Telephone and broadband	£370

Advertising and promotion	£2,420
Van	£3,235
Professional fees	£0
Rent	£2,500
Other	£0
Loan payments	£0
Total overheads	£10,063

Calculate the sales you need, in order to break even – your overheads in pounds, divided by your gross profit margin, times one hundred.

Breakeven figure = £25,868

Divide this figure by twelve, to calculate your monthly breakeven figure.

Monthly breakeven figure = £2,155

Calculate your net profit for the year in pounds, together with your net profit margin.

Projected sales	£88,850
Minus breakeven figure	£25,868
Balance	£62,982
Multiply by gross profit	38.9%

margin (%)	
Net profit in pounds	£24,500
Divide the net profit by your sales and multiply by one hundred	
Net profit margin =	27.6%

Out of the maze – appendix sixteen

BREAKEVEN AND PROFIT MARGINS: SHEET THREE – YOUR CALCULATIONS

First calculate your gross profit for the year:

Projected sales		£
Minus direct costs: Materials Labour		£ £
Total direct costs		£
Gross profit in pounds		£

Calculate your gross profit margin – your gross profit in pounds, divided by your sales in pounds, times one hundred. Gross profit margin =   %

Calculate your overheads for the year, prior to calculating your breakeven figure.

Heat, light and power	£
Printing and stationery	£
Insurance	£
Telephone and broadband	£

Advertising and promotion	£
Van	£
Professional fees	£
Rent	£
Other	£
Loan payments	£
Total overheads	£

Calculate the sales you need, in order to break even – your overheads in pounds, divided by your gross profit margin, times one hundred.

Breakeven figure = £

Divide this figure by twelve, to calculate your monthly breakeven figure.

Monthly breakeven figure = £

Calculate your net profit for the year in pounds, together with your net profit margin.

Projected sales	£
Minus breakeven figure	£
Balance	£
Multiply by gross profit	

margin (%)	
Net profit in pounds	£
Divide the net profit by your sales and multiply by one hundred	
Net profit margin =	%

Out of the maze – appendix sixteen

Breakeven and profit margins exercise – explanatory notes

- Projected sales: this figure is made up of cash sales totalling £17,250 together with the total credit sales generated, which will include those sales made in June i.e. £63,500 plus £8,100 = £71,600.
- Materials: these are calculated to be 40% of your sales total – so £88,850 x 40% = £35,540. Some of the material will have not been paid for as yet, however this total cost has been incurred in the production of the product.
- Labour costs: the total of £18,700 has been incurred in the production of the product.
- When the costs of materials and labour have been added together, the total direct costs amount to £54,240; when this figure is subtracted from the sales, this leaves a gross profit figure in pounds of £34,610.
- Gross profit margin: this is calculated by dividing the gross profit figure of £34,610 by the total sales of

£88,850 and multiplying by one hundred. (34,610 ÷ 88,850 x 100 = 38.9% to one decimal point.)

- Heat, light and power: costs totalling £450 have been incurred.

- Printing and stationery: costs totalling £560 have been incurred.

- Insurance: costs totalling £528 have been incurred.

- Telephone and broadband: costs totalling £370 have been incurred.

- Advertising and promotion: costs totalling £2,420 have been incurred – the first advertisement was placed in August i.e. that is eleven months of advertising.

- Van: costs totalling £2,400 have been incurred since September, to which have been added the costs of road tax, insurance and tyres giving a total of £3,235.

- Professional fees: no costs have been incurred in the first year.

- Rent: this costs £250 per month – the unit has been rented since September, so ten months rental has been incurred.

- Other: no other costs have been incurred.

- Loan payments: no costs have been incurred.

- Breakeven: the overheads total £10,063, so this figure divided by the gross profit margin of 38.9%, multiplied by one hundred, gives a breakeven figure of £25,868. (10,063 ÷ 38.9 x 100 = 25,868.) The monthly breakeven figure is simply the annual breakeven of £25,868 divided by twelve. Note: in this instance you could divide by ten, the number of active months, to give a more realistic figure.

- Net profit: this has been arrived at by subtracting the annual breakeven figure from the total sales, giving a balance of £62,982; this figure was then multiplied by the gross profit percentage of 38.9 to give a final figure of £24,500.

  (62,982 x 38.9 = 24,500.)
- Net profit margin: this has been arrived at by dividing the net profit figure of £24,500 by the total sales of £88,850 and multiplying by one hundred.

  (24,500 ÷ 88,850 x 100 = 27.6%)

So to summarise: the gross profit figure for the year in pounds works out at £34,610 or 38.9% of sales; the net profit for the year in pounds works out at £24,500 or 27.6% of sales, while the breakeven figure for the year amounts to £25,868.

Out of the maze – appendix seventeen

THE PROFIT AND LOSS FORECAST (AND EXERCISE)

As with the cashflow forecast, there are some principles or guidelines you should bear in mind when creating your profit and loss forecast; again these are reflected in the example exercise.

- Unlike the cashflow forecast, the profit and loss forecast (or statement) is not time sensitive; in fact, it is time defined in that it covers a specific trading period. For example, if your trading year runs from the beginning of April to the following March, then you will include all the sales you expect to generate (or have generated) within that period, whether or not you will be or have been paid in that time. Similarly, you will include all of the costs you expect to incur (or have incurred) in generating your sales within that period, whether or not you have paid the bills for the goods or services supplied. This calculation gives you a true picture as to whether you can sell your product or service for more money that it costs to make or deliver it and therefore whether it is profitable i.e. there is a surplus of income over expenditure.

- If you are VAT registered, then you will exclude any VAT from your figures. As a VAT registered business you are collecting this tax and passing it on to HMRC, therefore it will not be included in your figures when calculating your profit or loss, as in the long run it is not part of your sales or costs. On the other hand, if you are not VAT registered your figures will include any VAT you have had to pay but cannot offset and therefore has been passed on to your customers through inclusion in your costings.

- If you are a sole trader or partner you will not include any drawings you will take or have taken as they are not an allowable expense; your drawings will come out of any profit you make. Your profit is therefore shown as 'net profit before drawings'. On the other hand, if your business is a limited company, you will include your salary along with that paid to any staff, under the heading of wages, salaries or PAYE.

- Depreciation (see glossary) will never appear within your cashflow, as it is not 'real money'; however, depreciation will be included within your profit and loss as it can be offset against your sales, thus reducing your net profit and in turn, your tax liability. *For the purpose of this exercise you should assume any depreciation is at the rate of 20%.* Please note: if you are in any doubt as to how depreciation might affect your decisions when it comes to purchasing assets or how it might affect your tax liability, you should speak to an accountant.

- Although it is not relevant for this exercise, if you were to draw up a profit and loss forecast broken down over twelve months, you would apportion your costs. For example, if you were to spend £600 on insurance and pay for it outright, you would show that figure as a one-off payment in your cashflow in the month when the payment was made; however, the insurance covers twelve months not just the payment month – each month must carry its fair share of the cost, therefore you would put a figure of £50 in each month shown within your profit and loss.

The exercise.

As with the cashflow and breakeven exercises, there are three sheets provided for this exercise; firstly, a blank profit and loss for you to fill in using the figures and information contained within the cashflow (appendix nine) together with the breakeven and profit margins exercise (appendix sixteen). Secondly, a completed sheet to enable you to check your calculations and thirdly another blank sheet for use in creating your own forecast; please bear in mind that there is no standard format, however, the one provided is a perfectly workable template. Again, to avoid unnecessary complication, please assume that you are not VAT registered in this case and therefore all the figures will be gross figures. Please also assume that you are a sole trader.

Out of the maze – appendix seventeen

PROFIT AND LOSS FORECAST: SHEET ONE – BLANK

Cash sales	£
Cash from credit sales	£
Total sales	£
Less direct costs: Materials Labour	 £ £
Total direct costs	£
Gross profit (sales minus direct costs)	£
Gross profit margin (GP ÷ sales x 100)	%
Less overheads: Heat, light and power	 £

Printing and stationery	£
Insurance	£
Telephone and broadband	£
Advertising and promotion	£
Van	£
Professional fees	£
Rent	£
Other	£
Loan payments	£
Depreciation	£
Total overheads	£
Net profit before drawings (GP minus overheads)	£
Net profit margin (NP ÷ sales x 100)	%

Out of the maze – appendix seventeen

PROFIT AND LOSS FORECAST: SHEET TWO– ANSWERS

Cash sales	£17,250
Cash from credit sales	£71,600
Total sales	£88,850
Less direct costs: Materials Labour	£35,540 £18,700
Total direct costs	£54,240
Gross profit (sales minus direct costs)	£34,610
Gross profit margin (GP ÷ sales x 100)	38.9%
Less overheads: Heat, light and power	£450

Printing and stationery	£560
Insurance	£528
Telephone and broadband	£370
Advertising and promotion	£2,420
Van	£3,235
Professional fees	£0
Rent	£2,500
Other	£0
Loan payments	£0
Depreciation	£888
Total overheads	£10,951
Net profit before drawings (GP minus overheads)	£23,659
Net profit margin (NP ÷ sales x 100)	26.6%

Out of the maze – appendix seventeen

PROFIT AND LOSS FORECAST: SHEET THREE – YOUR CALCULATIONS

Cash sales	£
Cash from credit sales	£
Total sales	£
Less direct costs: Materials Labour	 £ £
Total direct costs	£
Gross profit (sales minus direct costs)	£
Gross profit margin (GP ÷ sales x 100)	%
Less overheads: Heat, light and power	 £

Printing and stationery	£
Insurance	£
Telephone and broadband	£
Advertising and promotion	£
Van	£
Professional fees	£
Rent	£
Other	£
Loan payments	£
Depreciation	£
Total overheads	£
Net profit before drawings (GP minus overheads)	£
Net profit margin (NP ÷ sales x 100)	%

Out of the maze – appendix seventeen

PROFIT AND LOSS EXERCISE – EXPLANATORY NOTES

- Total sales: this figure represents the total sales expected to be generated from the start of trading and includes the value of any invoices which may still be awaiting payment.
- Materials: this figure represents the amount expected to be spent on materials in order to be able to generate the total sales – this cost of materials is stated to be 40% of sales. The figure includes the value of any invoices which may still be awaiting settlement.
- Labour: this figure represents the amount of money spent on the payroll since taking on the member of staff.
- Gross profit: this is simply the total sales minus the total direct costs.
- Gross profit margin: this figure is calculated by dividing the gross profit of £34,610 by the total sales of £88,850 and multiplying by one hundred.
  (34,610 ÷ 88,850 x 100 = 38.9%)
- Overheads: these are calculated as set out in the Explanatory Notes for Appendix Sixteen – profit and loss exercise; these total £10,063 not including depreciation, which would need to be added for the purpose of this exercise.
- Depreciation: two capital items, a computer and van, are shown as being purchased during the year, worth £4,440 at the time of purchase; assuming depreciation

on these items is 20%, this would give an allowance of £888. (4440 x 20%) thus reducing the value of these assets to £3,552 at the year end. This also assumes that both items have been used exclusively for the business.

- Net profit: this is simply the gross profit minus the total overheads (which includes depreciation). Sole traders and partners would be taxed on this net profit figure of £23,659, whether they have taken this in drawings or not; for a limited company this figure would be the starting point for calculating any liability for corporation tax.

- Net profit margin: this figure is calculated by dividing the net profit of £23,659 by the total sales of £88,850 and multiplying by one hundred.
  $(23,659 \div 88,850 \times 100 = 26.6\%)$

Please note: there will be a slight discrepancy between the figures shown in the breakeven and profit margins exercise and the profit and loss exercise, as the gross profit percentage of 38.9 has been calculated to one decimal point only.

Out of the maze – appendix eighteen

PRICING – FACTORS TO CONSIDER

There are many factors which could influence the prices you charge; here are some of them:

- The number of advantages your product or service offers compared with those of your competitors, together with the appeal of your USP.
- How well your product works or your service delivers.
- How easy you make it for your customers to deal with you.
- How reliable and consistent are you and your product or service.
- Your style, packaging and presentation.
- The strength of your reputation and image.
- How your product looks – good design shines through.
- Your customer care – is it genuine or 'lip service'?
- Location – how convenient is it for your customers?
- Scarcity – the law of supply and demand.
- How far ahead of your competition you are.
- The degree of skill, knowledge and training that is involved in the production or delivery of your product or service.
- Whether your product or service can be described as luxury, basic or par for the course.
- Your pricing structure – must it encourage repeat business and/or larger orders?

- How good you are at resolving complaints or problems.
- How long it takes to make your product.
- Whether any guarantee or backup you provide is meaningful.
- The amount of 'hassle' you may encounter.
- The amount of profit you must make in order to grow your business.
- Whether you need to 'get a foot in the door'.
- Whether you need money quickly, in order to pay your bills.

Take stock of your strengths when compared to your competitors; if overall you offer more to your customers than your competition, then you will charge as much as them if not more. If you have some catching up to do, you will charge less.

To download all the forms and tables in Out of the maze,

as well as a working cash flow forecast, visit

www.outofthemaze.biz/book-downloads

and use the password "churchill" (all lower case)

www.ingramcontent.com/pod-product-compliance
Lightning Source LLC
Chambersburg PA
CBHW051531170526
45165CB00002B/694